Words that Sing

Sunrise Valley Elementary School

Copyright © 2011 by Sunrise Valley Elementary School

10824 Cross School Road

Reston, VA 20191

Phone: 703-715-3800

Principal: Dr. Elizabeth English

Assistant Principal: Mrs. Carol Burns

All rights in the intellectual property contained herein are reserved by Sunrise Valley Elementary School. Printed in the United States of America. Unless otherwise noted, no part of this publication may be reproduced, stored in a retrieval system, or transmitted in any form or by any means, electronic, mechanical, photocopying, recording, or otherwise, without the prior written permission of the publisher.

Contents

Preface v

Multi-Grade Class K–1
Ms. Robinson 1

Kindergarten
Ms. Scheufele—AM 3
Ms. Scheufele—PM 7

First Grade
Ms. Goveas-Foti 11
Mrs. Holland 15
Mrs. Marik 19

Second Grade
Mrs. Barna 23
Mrs. Bowser 29
Mrs. Cantillana 35
Mrs. Harris 41

Multi-Grade Class 2–4
Ms. Bamberger 27

Multi-Grade Class 2–3
Ms. Jacobs 39
Ms. Bursk 45

Third Grade
Mr. Kidder 47
Ms. Raphael 51
Ms. Robles-McCormack 57

Fourth Grade
Ms. Booth 63
Mrs. Crisafi 69
Mrs. Gualtieri 75
Mrs. Soliday 81

Fifth Grade

Mrs. Giovanini...87
Mr. Huffer..95
Ms. Leonard...103
Mr. Montaquila..113

Multi-Grade Class 4–6

Ms. Burkman...119

Sixth Grade

Ms. Diebold..121
Mrs. Kunkle..129
Mr. Parker...135
Mrs. Rossbach...147

Preface

The Sunrise Valley Poetry Anthology, *Words that Sing*, is an annual project of the students from Sunrise Valley Elementary School. It is an opportunity for all students to share, develop their imagination and creativity, and give voice to their thoughts, dreams, and lives through writing and artwork. Our student writers read as well as compose various forms of poetry such as cinquain, haiku, tanka, narrative, limericks, and most importantly, free verse. This gives students unique opportunities to express themselves and explore the intricacies of language and ideas. Illustrations to accompany the poems are explored in art class, where students have the opportunity to visually express the concepts in their poems. Many of these drawings have been included here along with the poems. This combination of poetry and art is grouped by grade and classroom.

Every year the students look forward to receiving their copy of the Anthology. It is our pleasure to provide the 6th edition of *Words that Sing*, and we hope you enjoy this collection of more than 600 poems, which gives each student at Sunrise Valley ES an opportunity to shine!

Sunrise Valley Elementary School Students and Staff
Reston, Virginia
June 2011

Multi-Grade Class K–1
Ms. Robinson

Kalina
K ute!
A dventurous
L oving
I nterested in piano
N ever frowning
A lways eating chips

By Kalina Ramarolahy

Shruti
S assy
H appy in school
R esponds to music
U nderstands movement
T alks with her eyes
I ncredible

By Shruti Chappidi

Gabby
G aba Gaba
A dventurous
B eats to her own drum
B each girl
Y oung star

By Gabriella Hao

Krushi
K ind
R ed dog
U ses eyes to communicate
S weet
H appy with sounds
I nterested in music

By Krushi Chepuri

Olivia
O utgoing
L aughing
I ntriguing
V ery theatrical
I ncredible
A lways loving

By Olivia Vascio

Morning Kindergarten

Ms. Scheufele

Dogs

Dogs like to swim.
Dogs like to play.
Dogs like to snuggle.
Dogs like to bark.
Beckham!

By Isak Danielsson

Moon

The moon was shining.
The star was shining.
The sun was shining.

By Gavin Lee

Hamburgers Falling Out of the Sky

Once there was hamburger that fell
Out of the sky.
We caught it
And it was yummy!

By Aidan Coughlin

Easter

Easter Bunny,
Easter Eggs,
Easter Candy,
Easter Presents,
I love Easter!

By Morgan Sivak

Flowers

Roses are beautiful.
Iris are white.
Bluebells are blue.
Flowers smell good.

By Paras Bhanot

Swimming

I am swimming in the pool.
I am jumping in the water.
I see the toy underwater
And I see another toy!

By Agata Gorski

Happy Birthday

I am Naomi!
I hope it is my birthday.
I hope everybody comes to my party.
And I get a lot of presents today!

By Naomi Kishimoto

Kittens Meow

Two little kittens were meowing,
Happily!
And then two little kittens saw
A ghost!
OOOOOOOOOOOOOOO!
MEOW! MEOW! MEOW!
Then the ghost went away!

By Juliana Cox

Cats

Cats are going on the grass.
There is so much to do.
The cats are playing
In the backyard.
Slipping,
Sliding,
Having so much fun!

By Anna Stoops

Rainbow

After the rain,
A rainbow came out,
And a flower came out!

By Matthew Mitrani

The Birthday

Fun is when it is your birthday!
Today is the birthday.
The birthday has come to you.
I have a birthday.
Everyone has a birthday.
Everyone has a fun day!

By Maggie Thomas

Flowers & Rainbows

Flowers and rainbows are alike.
When it rains flowers appear
And rainbows start to appear too.
Wouldn't it be neat if flowers
Grew on rainbows!

By Zia Wallach

The Flowers Bloom

I see a butterfly, safely flying by.
I see flowers bloom,
Red and Green!

By Nick Darmory

Ghost

The ghost likes to scare people away.
But the police took him away.
He got away!
The police got him again!

By Mason Duprey

Penguins

The penguins were sliding on the ice.
They fell in the water!
Splash!

By Benji Petinaux

Puppies

Puppies are cute,
And fun,
And snugly,
And nice as playmates.
And they always want to
Go to school with you!

By Allie Harris

Lions

I have this little lion,
That loves to do science.
His uncle loves to read to him
Stories about lions.

By Luke Smiley

Pink Princess

Princesses like pink.
Do you like pink?
I love pink!
Did you know that bunnies,
Ears are pink, on the inside.
Princesses like bunnies!

By Laurie Smith

The Dog

The is dog is trying to get
Out of the rain.
Rain, rain, rain!
Now the dog finds a dry spot!

By Brenna Scanlan

Spring

The flowers grow.
The birds sing.
The butterflies fly in the sky.
The leaves grow on the trees.
The sky is blue!

By Claire Wang

Swordfish

A swordfish swam to the boat.
People are on the boat making kabobs.
The swordfish jumped up!
Got the kabob…
And ate it!

By Cameron Parsa

Kindergarten

I love kindergarten!
It is fun.
We sing.
We learn.
We write poems.
School is awesome!

By Rachel March

Sharks

Sharks are evil.
Sharks are bad.
Sharks are gray.
Sharks eat fish.
Sharks live in the sea.

By Jakey Nguyen

Money

Money is for buying stuff.
Lots of stuff…
TOYS!

By Erik Molnar

The Star Fell Out of the Sky

I saw a star fall out of the sky.
We became friends.
We played with each other.
We need some bricks.
Then we can build a house.

By Allison Torres

Spiders

Spiders crawling to eat food.
He sees a person…..
Crunch!
Run!

By Jack Koester

Princesses Love

Princesses love dogs,
And cats,
And bunnies,
And they love and love
And love and love!

By Cary Green

Ninjago

Ninjagos are so cool!
I like my Ninjagos.
I love Ninjagos!

By Matthew Mirabello

Afternoon Kindergarten
Ms. Scheufele

Star
The stars are in the sky.
They shine at night.
They are yellow and bright.
By Cecilia Aparicio

The Fox
Once upon a time there was a fox.
The fox went to look for food.
He looked until he found food.
Then he went back home.
By David Aguilera

The Brontosaurus
Once a brontosaurus ate me
But I jumped out!
I said, "Ha, ha, ha!'
And I ran away.
The end.
By Toby Smith

Rainbow
Rain…
It stopped raining.
The sun came out.
I saw a rainbow.
I am happy!
By Sarah Wickman

Doggie
The doggie was hungry.
She wanted to eat
But her snack ran away.
By Selin Altunyay

I Love You
I love you, Mommy!
You love me!
You play games with me.
You let me cook.
You hug me.
You kiss me.
Love.
Love.
Love.
By Ryan Terry

Kittens
Kittens are cute.
They are black.
They are white.
They are brown.
They are everywhere.
By Zoe Pilon

Zekrom
Zekrom is trying to use
His electric powers.
But they were out!
By Evan Rosenblatt

My Birthday

I love my birthday
Because you get to have a cake!
You will have fun!
It is my birthday!

By Leo Hunt

Monkeys

Monkeys are fun.
And I love them.
They have brown tails.
They live in the jungle.

By Justin Shuman

The Lobster

It will pinch you and me.
It will pinch you, silly.
Stop! Red, pink, purple,
Blue feathered duck, stop!
Don't pinch him! He is safe now!

By Carter Liggett

Monsters

The monsters were just settling down.
But when they sat down…
SNAP!
A crab snapped their PJs in two.
I found a tree.
Good night, monsters!

By James Harriot

The Rainbow

I saw a rainbow.
I saw the rain.
I saw the sun.
I saw the clouds.
I love it!

By Amaya Pegues

Shark

A shark in the ocean
Was swimming
With its mouth open
Trying to catch the baby fish.

By Akash Boinpally

My Family

They love me.
I love them.
My family is the best in the world!
I really like my family.

By Lilah Skoy

The Umbrella Ocean

The man wants to ride on top of the sea.
And he wants to go past high tide
And low tide.
He will go past sea tide but don't forget—
He also has to glide out!
He has to sail now. Let him go now.
But he has to pick up a cow back in the sea
storm and then go back into the water.

By Max Daum

Angels

Angels protect you.
Angels are cool.
They fly.
They are God's friends.
Are they real? Yes!

By Lexy Pak

Super Star

Super Star
Blew up.
Mario was furious.
It is a fun game to play!

By Sam Garnett

Bill

Box boy. Box girl.
Box man. Boxes.
Nooooo! Oh, no!
Bill gets eaten. Poor Bill!

By Josh Garnett

The Rainbow

It was a rainy day.
Too wet to go outside.
I played with my toys.
As I was playing with my toys,
Suddenly a rainbow came out.
I am playing outside now!

By Mary Marzouka

The Dog

Stop, Dog! Go to Mommy's car!
Stop, Dog! Go to Mommy's car!
Stop, Dog! Go to Mommy's car!
Stop, Dog! CAR!!!
Good job!

By Avi Steppel

The Crab

The crab is on the beach.
The crab is scurrying
On the side of the beach.
He is playing hide-and seek
With his crab friends hiding
In sea shells.
It is fun!

By Henry Gill

The Shark and the Chipmunk

The shark was chasing the chipmunk
Because he wanted to tag the chipmunk. They
wanted to jump in the water and they wanted to
swim in the water together.

By Suya Haering

The Crab

The crab is walking sideways
on the beach.
The crab is my brother.
The crab ceremony is today.
They are happy!

By Abe Thomas

The Crab

The crabs are on the beach.
They are walking on the beach again!
They love swimming.
They love the sun.
I love swimming too!

By Kaitlin Mahon

The Zoo

What do you see at the zoo?
Monkeys. Ooh, ooh!
Crocodiles. Snap, snap!
Sheep. Baa, baa!
Goats and turtles!

By Christian McIntyre

Dogs and Puppies

Dogs and puppies are cute.
And they cuddle and lick.
That's the cuteness of puppies and dogs.
And they love you!
And they love to take a walk with you!

By Marley Ward

First Grade
Ms. Goveas-Foti

Flowers

Roses are read
Violets are blue
But most of all
I love mom!

By Annie Abruzzo

Turtles

Turtles are cute
Turtles are friendly
You can have a turtle as a pet
I love turtles!
Turtles
Turtles
Turtles!

By Gwyneth Wagner

I'm at the Park

I see green grass
I see purple flowers
I see yellow sun
I like to go to the park

By Stephanie Rajab

School

School is fun
School is funny
I like school
School!

By Habibah Sharaf

Horses

Horses are nice
Horses are fast
You can ride them
They are black, white,
brown and gray
and all different colors
I love horses

By Riley Lender

The Word Wall

And, are, after, because, come, can, could, dear, down, eat, friends, from, here, have, like, my, me, make, our, other, of, over, play, put, ravenous, said, saw, should, special, school, the, this, that, they, there, up, under, valentine, were, who, will, would, went, we, when, with, you
Are all on the word wall

By Shannon Gallagher

Bubbles Bubbles Bubbles

Bubbles
Bubbles
Drifting through the air
Bubbles
Bubbles
Drift without a care
Bubbles
Bubbles
Pop!
Goodbye bubbles

By Allison McBride

The Cat
The cat meowed
Then he ate
Crunch
Crunch
Crunch
And then he slept
ZZZZZZZZZ
And woke up
Yawn
By Griffin Van Hilst

Hayley
Happy
Awesome
Yay
Laugh
Excited
Yelly
By Reagan Palik

Blue
Blue is the color of the sky
The color of rain
Blue is the color of sadness
And the color of tears
Blue is awesome!
By Nick DiCintio

Moms Are Nice
Moms are nice
Mom is smart
Mom is funny
By Christina Simon

Chicks
I see cute chicks
I feel the softness of their fur
I smell the farm
I hear the baby chicks chirping
Chirp!
Chirp!
Chirp!
By Catherine Evans

Flowers Grow
Flowers grow
In the sun
With blooming
And sparkling
By Benham Cobb

Volcanoes
Volcanoes go boom!
Burning lava
Melting the city
By Gareth Leonard

Signore Ant
He has Mexican antennae
He has been on many adventures
By Rian Fisher

Red
Red is hot lava
Red is blood
Red lips
Red is Super S's
By Dylan Mulvaney

My Dad
He is funny
He is good
He is good at doing laundry
He is nice
He is good at video games
By Brian Ball

My Sisters
Moira is weird
Moira is two
Liliana is annoying
Moira is too
Liliana is jealous
Moira is like a soldier
I am loving like my sisters!
By Grace McInelly

Kit Kat
Crunch
Crunch
Crunch
Yum
Yum
Kit Kat is yummy!
It smells like chocolate
It tastes like peanut butter
It feels like an eraser
And it looks like a bar
Me love Kit Kat!
By Hayley Greene

Popcorn
Popcorn is tasty
Popcorn is sweet
I like popcorn
Popcorn
Popcorn
Popcorn!
By Justin Vogel

My Brothers
I have a brother
I have two
I have a big brother who is 13
And a brother who is 1
I love both my brothers
By Essex Finney

Lollipop
Mmmmm
The lollipop is yummy
I got the blue one
It tastes like blueberry
Loli
Loli
Pop!
By Kylie Hughes

Red
Rose red
Blood red
Sunset red
Ruby red
Cheek red
Love red
By Manda Xie

The Green
There are green trees
There are green leaves
There are green shirts
There is green ink
There is green grass
There is green everything
By Matthew Silverio

The Sun
The sun is a shiny thing
The sun shines on my feet
The sun dries me
The sun glows over me
By Abigail Manalansan

First Grade
Mrs. Holland

Candy

Candy is sweet
And colorful!
I love candy!
My favorite is
Starburst!
I wish I could have it
All the time!
What's your favorite candy?

By Mari Huff

Candy

Kit Kats,
Smarties,
Jelly Beans,
Musketeers,
Milky Ways,
Nestle Crunch,
I like candy!

By Gretel Brown

Waterfalls

Waterfalls
Pouring towards
Me!!!
Water fills the
Air!
The sun makes the
Water warm!
Waterfalls, waterfalls!

By Kathleen Le

Spring

Spring is nice,
Spring is cool,
I like the name,
Do you?
I love spring like
I love you!

By Mia Nguyen

I Love My Mommy

I like my Mommy,
Just like salami,
I like her because,
She is sweet,
Just like candy,
I love my Mommy,
So, so, really, really,
Very, very much!
She is the best!

By Sara Shahzad

NHL

It is awesome and cool!
I do not play it,
But I watch it!
You shoot,
You score!
Goal!
It is cool and awesome!
WHOOO, HOOO!

By Will Giery

Soccer

Soccer is cool!
It makes me happy!
I love Soccer!
I would like to play
Soccer!

By Nolan Balducci

Bunnies

Bunnies are fast,
Bunnies are cute,
I love bunnies!
Bunnies are the best
Animals I have ever seen!

By Juana Hernandez

Legos

Legos are cool
And fun to play with!
You can build anything
With them!

By Rohan Mudras

Frogs

Hip, Hop, Hippity Hop,
Hip, Hop, Hippity Hop,
Frogs are hopping
Around the shop!
Hip, Hop, Hippity Hop!

By Katie Harris

My Mom Is

My mom is the coolest!
She is as cool as a pair of shades!
My mom is as pretty as a
Princess!
My mom is as sweet as ice cream!
My mom is as athletic as a dog!
I love my mom!

By Hannah Clements

Gravity Crash

I love gravity crash.
It is my favorite video game.
I like multiplayer and
Single player!
I'm at the fifth galaxy!
It's the last one!
I beat four bosses!

By Aidan Cross

I am a Little Girl

I like myself with my hat,
I like myself when I go to school,
I like myself at my house,
I like myself at the park!
I am a little girl!
I like myself

By Eunice Williams

Waterfalls

Water is refreshing,
You can feel the beat,
Like a record player,
SHHHH goes the water!
SPLASH!
Glub, glub, glub,
Goes the fish,
Relaxing waterfalls,
The falls are sweet like . . .
The Earth!
We're falling,
BANG! SPLASH!

By Lainey Miller

Galaxies

I like Galaxies,
I don't like the middle,
Because there is a
In the middle of the galaxy!

By Alex Randerson

Mario and Luigi

Mario and Luigi
Always
Win in
Mario Brothers,
Mario Galaxy 1,
Mario Galaxy 2,
Mario Galaxy 3,
I love Mario and Luigi

By Caden Green

Seagulls

The seagulls dive into the water,
Flying above the ocean,
They screech
And fly,
And dive,
Screech, Screech,
Bye, bye!

By Joey Brotemarkle

Football

New York Giants is the best!
The Super Bowl is the best!
The Packers win!
Be careful,
But try your best!
Tackle!

By Jack Woods

Fish

I love my fish!
I eat them!
No, don't eat them!
They're my fish!
You told me you ate them!
I did,
I was joking!

By Brien Nelson

Basketball

Basketball is so fun!
I like basketball!
I am so good at it!
Because you can shoot it in
The hoop and say,
Shoot!
2 POINTS!

By Bannon Brazell

Volcanoes

Volcanoes are brown and red,
They are bigger than you!
EXPLODE!

By Abdallah Elmuhtaseb

Intrepid

Intrepid,
Intrepid,
It's a carrier,
It goes to outer sea
For combat!
I love Intrepid!

By Mick Ball

Bunnies

Bunnies are cute,
They hop everywhere,
They are,
Cute, cute, cute!
Bunnies are cool!

By Caytlin Velarde

Starry Skies

Starry skies
Make me feel good!,
I love to look at the stars,
There are so many
Stars, stars!!!

By Emily Slater

First Grade
Mrs. Marik

Rain
Rain
Comes
Down
Sun comes up
A rainbow comes after!
By Alana Pudner

Vanilla
Vanilla
Funny
Fragile
Class pet
Vanilla
By Danielle Elliott

People
People can be any color
Some people are nice
Some people are poor
Some people are rich
But almost all of us are
Good enough!
By Sarah Rajab

Spiky Plants
Spiky plants
As sharp as a chainsaw
"Ouch", said the finger.
By Quin Kelly

Splash
Water.
A frog
Jumps in.
The sound of water.
By Carson Owen

My Brother
I love my brother
His name is Spencer
He has autism
I love him
By Abby Brenner

Horses
Horses can run
People like horses
Horses like people
You can ride a horse
Some horses are wide
Some are tame
I like horses!
By Michaela Hodges-Fulton

Spring
Spring is very, very filled with pollen
I am allergic
I go outside and
SNEEZE!
By Abigail Brenner

Growing

I
I a
I am
I am g
I am gr
I am gro
I am grow
I am growi
I am growin
I am growing
I am growing s
I am growing sl
I am growing slo
I am growing slow
I am growing slowl
I am growing slowly

By Jaden Kritsky

SVES

SVES
Is the best,
So I am loving it!

By Krishan Shah

Ducks

Ducks are quacky,
They are soft
I like ducks
And
I hope you do too.
By Nora Colvin
Submarines
Stealth
Sneaky
Devastating
Going up
Going down
Cool

By Christopher Kosowiec

The Big Sea

The big sea is as big as 80 old islands
That are 80 miles wide
It is a beautiful sight when the
Sun is shining
After the sunset is over
The ocean stays calm
The big ocean is blue
I am tired
It's time for the ocean to go to bed.

By Aaron Dubois

Lefty the Cat

Lefty likes to snack
Lefty likes to sleep
Lefty likes to play
I like Lefty

By Mamadou Ndiaye

Spring

The clouds were
moving
The sun was
Blowing
The flowers were
Blooming
The grass was
Growing

By Jada Carter

The Sun

Here comes the sun
Here comes the sun
In the summer sky
So, so bright laying in the sky
Right there
So bright up there
Here comes the sun
Here comes the sun

By Gavin Anthony

Books
Books
Plant books and
Cooking books and
Learning books and
Animal books and
Fiction books and
Non-fiction books and
Silly books and
Iron man books
Marvel books and
Library books and
Candy books and
House books
Great friend books
Amazing books
YAA books
By Kyle Boo

The Earth
Earth is cool
Earth is fun
Earth is our planet
Earth is amazing
Earth is even more amazing
I live on earth
By Isky Davis

SVES
SVES
Is the best,
So I am loving it!
By Krishan Shah

Working with the Wheat
The boy is getting tired
Still a lot of work to do
The poor little boy thinks he is alone
He sees the sun coming up.
By Jake Edwards

Friends
I have lots of them
I like my friends
They are all nice
And I
Am too!
By Sydney Hahn

Easter
There are a lot of
Eggs
On
Easter
There is an
Easter Bunny
Easter is on April 24th
By Shriya Vavilala

Chicks
Chicks are as cute as a puppy
Their feathers are as
yellow as a school bus
By Emma Dettra

My Family
I love my family
They are great
I play with my cousin sometimes
I am going to
RED LOBSTER
To celebrate my dad's birthday
He is turning 41!
By Byron Rivey

A Long-Necked Creature
Who could be that long-necked shadow
Behind me be?
Could it be ME?
It's a flamingo behind me!
By Ruby Heitmann

Second Grade
Mrs. Barna

Football
I am good at catching
I am good at juking
I catch the kickoff
I run with the football
People try to tackle me,
But I get away!
I feel good and proud
When I get a touchdown.
I get super, super happy!
By Nicky Mounkhaty

Paper Airplanes
Paper airplanes
High flying
Long distances
Different airplanes
Flying Ninjas
Paper Darts
They fly like soaring birds
With names like Headhunter
Spike
The Raptor
PAPER AIRPLANES!
By Matthew Fritz

Joy
Joy is as graceful as an angel
Joy is as gentle as a lamb
Joy is as stylish as a jar of sparkles
Joy is as friendly as a foal
Joy is as rich as a billionaire
Joy is as smart as a calculator
Joy is as tuneful as a song
Joy is my friend!
By Vanessa Hathaway

Rainbows
R is for red roses
A is for a lot of orange peels
I is for icy light
N is for not as much money
B is for blueberries
O is for outer space black
W is for wow purple
Rainbow words are magical,
But family is better!
By Audrey Webb

Art
I take my pencil
I think what to draw
I draw a person walking
Then I softly color the sunset
Mixing yellow and orange
I paint the sky light blue
Then I let it dry
I wait and wait
Then I think of another picture
in my head
I have so many things to draw!
By Joy Oh

Summer

I always like summer the best.
There's no school.
It's very hot.
We eat tacos outside.
We swim in the lake and the pool.
We go to Ocean City.
We make sand castles at the beach.
We swim in the cold ocean
We play Pac Man at the boardwalk
And my birthday is in the summer!
I love summer best.

By Sammy Deeds

Wrestling

Dripping with sweat
Fighting to win
Beating the opponent
Sometimes losing
Having energy at all times!

By Troy Elliot

In May

You can wear shorts
The pool opens
The sun comes out
We play and run and laugh
We run and play tag
I chase my friends and smile
And joy comes to us!

By Adrianna Smith

Cupcakes

Cupcakes
Sweet, delicious
Creamy, tasty, yummy
Cake, chocolate frosting with rainbow sprinkles
Little treats!

By Alaina Cordts

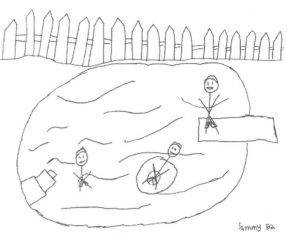

Summer

I always like summer
Because it is my birthday
We go camping
My family goes to the beach
And when I get in the water
Ho boy!
It is so cold.

By Nick Haitz

My Dog, Snowball

Who is the one who licks your cheeks?
Snowball!
Who is the one who runs in the kitchen?
Snowball!
Who is the one who annoys my dad?
Snowball!
Who is the one who gets a bone every day?
Snowball!
Who is the one I cuddle with?
Snowball!

By Sara Taber

Basketball

Basketball
Shooting hoops
Dribbling, running, winning
Happy to be playing!
Great game.

By Sam Constantine

Crazy Max
Max, Max
Crazy cat
Jump, play
Lose a toy
Run, run
Go upstairs
Come back down
Jump around
Max, Max
Crazy cat!

By Noah Lendman

Stars
Stars are as bright as the sun
As high as the sky
They are as yellow as ducklings
They are shaped like starfish
They look so fantastic way up there
They look down at us like God
I love shining stars so much!

By Athena Joannou

If You Fall
If you fall, it is okay.
Just put a band aid on it
It will be okay in two days
Then you can play
But just watch out
For a bump
Or something that can make you fall!!!
And don't run into a wall
Or a person
So watch out!!!

By Carter Plummer

Summer
I always like summer best
You get to take a long vacation
Going to the beach
Collecting shells
When you stick your feet in the water
Hooo it's so cold!

By Matthew Zheng

Turtles
Turtles
Slow, green
Eats in water
Blends in with the rocks
Hiding creatures

By Kerigan Lindmeier

In December
All the leaves fall down
It is getting very cold
That is the sign that Christmas is coming
We get hot cocoa
It is fun to watch T.V.
We make snowmen
And forts
We make snowballs
I love opening presents
December is my favorite month!

By Grace Mirabello

Rocks
I like rocks!
Crystals, quartz and gems
Rubies, emeralds and diamonds
Smooth rocks, round rocks
Everyone is different
Small ones, big ones
Meteorites and coal
One day I can be a geologist!

By Lauren Smiley

Happiness

Happiness is a big scoop of vanilla ice cream
With gummy bears (green ones)
Happiness is holding my cat
And she falls asleep on me
Happiness is snow days with two hour delays
Happiness is no school and we have hot cocoa
with marshmallows
And happiness is winning a basketball game by
one point!

By Brianna Scott

Basketball

Running, dribbling
Passing, Shooting
Basketball
It doesn't matter
If you win or lose
It just means you had fun
Three pointers
Dunks
Steals
Picks
Lay-ups
I love basketball!

By Andy Hurt

Busch Gardens

Busch Gardens is awesome
Because of all the rides
There is the second fastest ride
in the whole U.S.A.
My two favorite roller coasters
The Scorpion and the Cheetah
The Cheetah feels like I am
going in different angles
The Scorpion feels the same but so much faster!

By Reilly Lapine

Football

Down, set, hike
I run for the pass
I catch it
Yes!
I get tackled
No!
Second down
We are going to do a hand off
Ok, got it?
Yes!
Let's go then
Down, set, hike
The hand off is to #59
Go go!!!
Yes!
We got a touchdown!
We are kicking the ball now
They touched the ball
It is on the ground
Yes!
A fumble
We got it!
14 to 0
We won!
Yeeeeeesssssss!!!

By Aidan Scanlan

Summer

I always like summer best
You can go to the pool
You can have play dates
You don't go to school
You can see butterflies
You can read outside
You can have popsicles too
I always like summer best!

By Adelina Blas

Multi-Grade Class 2–4
Ms. Bamberger

Teddy Bear
Bear best toy, ever
I go to sleep with my bear.
THE END
By Alex Torres

kN ow how to fix 3PO
A monster is in my house
T hree PO is the best
E lephants are big
By Nate Gibson

    J umping Cat
    O utdoor Cat
Scratc H ing Cat
    iN door Cat
    W andering Cat
    A rching Cat
    pL aying Cat
    T iger Cat
    E xploring Cat
    R unning Cat
By John Walter Egan

K ite
A mazing
T rain
I ce cream
E gg
By Katie Meng

C hristian!
H ave a good night
I love to play "I got a feelin"
S inging is fun
T onight
"I got a feelin, woo-hoo"
A piano for me
N ow that's a magnifying glass
By Christian McIntyre

A nts are cool
L ikes to play with my dog
E ggs are yummy to eat
N ate is my friend
A wesome
By Alena Rinaldi

P laying with friends
H appy
I like Sider-Man The Series
L ego
I like books
P lay
By Philip Davis

Second Grade
Mrs. Bowser

Peas
They float into my mouth
like snow angels.
They're not monsters, aliens, or witches.
They're peas.
And whenever I eat
them I swallow with joy.
By Bethany Burke

The Paw
I get a treat.
I say "paw" to my dog
Lilly.
BANG!
Something hit me.
At least I still have
my treat.
Gobble gobble.
LILLY.
By Connor Novak

Three Kingdoms
Boom! Boom!
A thundering gallop of horses' feet.
As a big fight goes on.
Boom! Boom!
The Mongols are racing for more power.
The Chinese fight back!
They are the winners!
By Zack Kennedy

Airplane
An airplane is a racecar but
just flies in the sky.
An airplane has wings of a peacock
gliding in the sky.
An airplane is bigger if you just imagine.
An airplane can walk with
its tiny wheels.
Don't complain, you and an airplane
can be just the same.
By Mark Frucht

Moon
Way up in the gleaming ocean of stars
in the sparkling night of evil and good,
the moon lights up the night
with its glow like
a mountain of crystals
and diamonds.

Its midnight shine
gives me chills
as if I'm standing in the middle
of the polar ice.
When the sun comes out
the next day,
I say it's okay
because I will see
my wonderful friend
again tonight.
By Bryn Yenesel

The Dog Who Went to the Bathroom

Dogs dogs
They're so cool.
Dogs dogs
Oh! Noooo, mom!
The dog is going to
my bathroom!
Mom!
Flush now because
I have to clean
up.

By Kanz Abdulla

Video Games Are Fun

I got a new
video game.
It is super fun to play.
I can blow up trees.
Just like people!
And get some coins back.
If you are really bored,
and if your mom lets you,
just go and play
your video game.
And just so you know
what game I'm talking about,
it is Lego Battles
Ninjago!

By Billy Wessel

Moon

Moon, moon, moon,
The moon is fun.
Sometimes it is like a football
flying as tall as a bird.
Sometimes it is like a banana,
I want to eat that banana.
The moon has a friend.
Do you know who?

By Jack Wu

Guess

I'm sticky.
I feel icky.
My name is Nicky.
I'm tricky.
What am I?
No…
No…
YES!
I'm a…
Monster.

By Braden Ratcliffe

Tears

Tears rolling down my cheeks
it feels like a horse's feet
thumping on my cheeks.
But, wait. Why?
Why is there tears rolling down my cheeks?
Am I crying for joy
or am I sad or mad?
There it was.
It hit me.
I was crying for joy.
The angels had heard my cry.
Spring was finally here.

By Sam Harris

Dogs

Dogs are nice.
They feel as soft as a cloud.
They can be brown,
white,
gray,
and black too.
Woof!
I wish I had a dog
to play with all day long.

By Morin Nessim

Clouds

Clouds are like cotton balls
calmly drifting,
in the light blue sky.
When I see clouds
I think of cool shade
cooling me off.
When I look at them,
they look like monsters,
crocodiles and sometimes even
just random, weird things.
When they are dark
they make me think dark inside.

By Kaliyana Haering

Dogs

Dogs
Their ears like tall pointy bunny ears.
Some have floppy ears
which sort of camouflage to the dog.
Their bark is like a noisy song
to me.
Their tail is like
a fan which only swishes
when the dog is happy,
joyful or excited.

By Mika Ernst

Danger Frog

Danger!
Whap!
The powerful
umpire
said, "Attack!"
Frogs!
Toads!
Battle.

By Caleb Noll

Underground Cave

tip toe tip toe
animals are staring at me
stalagmites and stalactites
are reaching
for me
glowing
glistening
as
beautiful
as
can
be.

By Valeria Beauchamp

Hot Dogs

The bun feels soft in my hands.
I can feel the hot dog through the bug.
I squeeze the ketchup on the red
juicy hot dog.
It looks like a red snake.
I bite the hot dog.
It is so delicious.

By Jennifer Hogan

Big Fat Flying Hippopotamuses

What are big fat flying
hippopotamuses?
Flies!
I hate flies,
though I like that frogs eat them!
That is a secret from
FLIES!

By Isabella Nijkamp

The Feeling

My cheek is wet and soggy.
Rain is gushing down my face.
My eyes are boiling.
My heart is pounding.
Furious
Emotional
Sad
Touched
What's happening?
Then I hear a chirp.
I stop to listen.
The sun comes up.
I stop.
My tears are gone.

By KK Bennett

Beans

My mom says, "Come eat!"
I say, "So what's for dinner?"
She replies, "Beans."
"BEANS!" I said, "I HATE beans!"
And when I saw them, all I saw was
big, brown blobs of nothing,
or maybe a dump pile.
Because I think beans are gross, disgusting,
indescribable, ugly monsters.
"Maybe I should skip dinner,"
I said to myself.

By Everett Liggett

Frogs

Frogs, frogs, 1, 2, 3.
Everett likes frogs just like me.
Frogs are as cool as roller coasters.
Frogs are nice and there are many
different types.
And frogs are good just like me!

By Ritesh Shrivastav

People, People, PEOPLE!

People are staring at
me walking, running,
speeding, stop it, People!
Stop it, stop it!
People, People. People!
Thanks for the ice
cream cone
people!

By Aidan Habibi

Plants vs. Zombies

Aaaaah!
A zombie!
Put down a pie shooter.
He is dead.
Uh-oh! Football player zombie!
Put down the cherry bomb.
BOOM!!!
Uh-oh!
Scuba diver!
Put down the seaweed.
Uh-oh!
There's a zombie in a tractor!
Put down a squash.
BOOM!!!
Uh-oh!
It's a zombie in a robot!
He goes boom by the frozen watermelon!
By Zombie

By Drew Mouritzen

Under the Ocean

The sand as smooth as skin
and silky as water.
Dolphins splashing through
the ocean.
It sounds like
splash
splash
splash
The water is as clear as a mirror
and fish are wishing
through the water
and crabs are smashing their
claws against
the sand.
The seaweed is swishing through
the water.

By Maja Bradic

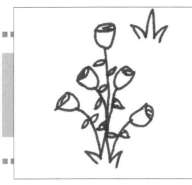

Second Grade
Mrs. Cantillana

Gymnastics
I love gymnastics.
It is so much fun!
I twirl.
I spin.
I do a split.
It is so much fun!
I leap.
I even go on the balance beam.
It is so much fun!
By Jayda Pak

First Day
I'm nervous.
It is my first day.
Everyone looked at me
Like I was a girl
With a bad hair day.
But then,
Throughout the day,
Everyone was nice.
I made a friend.
By Katie McMonagle

Chris
Chris is as strong as an elephant.
Chris is as funny as a circus clown.
Chris is as stubborn as a knot.
(Well, not anymore.)
By Michael Panatier

Skipping Rocks
Skip, Skip,
I go from rock to rock.
Uh, oh.
I'm losing my balance.
Jump, jump,
Splash!
Oh, no.
I fell in the water.
Quouk, quouk,
My feet are soaking.
There is water in my shoes.
Quouk, quouk, quouk.
That sound is so weird.
Quouk, quouk.
By Kyle Nobles

Crickets
Head,
Thorax,
Abdomen.
All right!
Chirp, chirp, chirp.
What was that?
Chirp, chirp,
Little creature coming by.
Who is it?
Crickets!
Chirp, chirp.
By Hima Bathula

Popcorn

As yellow as the butter it's made with,
And as yummy as a doughnut.
Pop, pop, pop!
As noisy as a giant's voice.
Boom, boom, boom!
And as fluffy as a bunny's tail.

By Karen Song

Love in My Heart

I look in the stars,
In my robe.
At night the world glows.

By Fouad Khatib

Memory Rocks

I remember the sand between my toes.
I remember collecting shells.
I remember some rocks in the water.
Memory of rocks.
Rocks, rocks,
Memory rocks.

By Julia France

Roller Coasters

Roller coasters,
Fun, scary,
Bumpy, moving, shaking,
Fast like lightning bolts,
Comet.

By Gabriel Levy

Popcorn

Popcorn popping,
One by one,
Popping like a kangaroo,
Pop, pop the popcorn goes.
"Wahoo!" they say as they jump.

By Sancho Calupitan

Bunnies

Bunnies,
Cute, loveable,
Running, eating, jumping,
Hopping around the world,
Boing!

By Jin Din

Snake in the Weeds

There once was a snake
I saw in the weeds.
Its body was like a shadow,
But its eyes were bright as angels.

By Zoey Hunt

Skateboard

Skateboard,
Cool designs,
Spinning, 360, flips,
Having fun all around,
Tricks.

By Brian Nguyen

I Read a Book

I read a book that was on my lap,
It had a page that made me laugh.
That night it made me dream happiness.

By Caley Duchak

My Dock
I'm standing on my dock.
I see the ripples on the water.
I think the time is dawn.
All my thoughts
are fading away from me.
By Abby Leary

Spiderman
Spiderman, Spiderman
does whatever a spider can.
Swings his web everytime,
Catch the feeling,
It's just like mine.
Look out!
Here comes the
Spiderman.
By Daris Rankins

Pac Man
Pac Man,
Yellow, black,
Crunching, moving, eating,
Always hungry for dots,
Exciting.
By Joseph Soifer

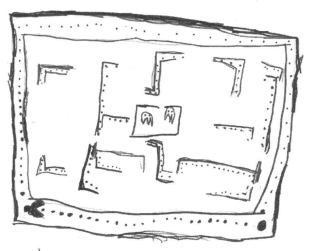

Football
Football
Tackle, catch,
Injury, fumble, interception,
Winning games,
Losing games,
Fun.
By Kado Kishimoto

Pyramids
Pyramids
Shiny, gold,
Huge, sand, bricks,
Mummies guarding the coins.
Egypt.
By Zander Thomas

Mom
As nice as a puppy,
As pretty as a butterfly,
As quiet as a dream,
As fast as a motorcycle,
As smart as a computer,
As caring as a doctor,
As cuddly as a teddy bear,
She is like my best friend.
By Kira Ketelhut

Mummies
Mummies, mummies,
Here and there.
Mummies, mummies,
Everywhere.
They are white as ancient toilet paper.
But don't release the curse.
By Ali Nilforoush

Tornadoes

Tornadoes in the air,
While people are on the ground.
I don't know what to do,
Maybe I should drink some stew.
I'm done with my stew,
I still don't know what to do.
Maybe I should check if the storm passed through.
I opened the door,
I put my feet on the floor,
I got sucked up from the tornado,
Maybe I should eat a tomato.

By Michael Flammang

Ode to a Hot Dog

Oh, how your mustard completes you.
Oh, how your dogness bark goes so loud that I can't even hear you.
Oh, how your buns are so fluffy.
Oh, how you're so yummy.
Oh, how your dog is so pink.
Your outsides are so hot.
Oh, how your whole thing is so intense.
Everything about you is 100% great.

By Alex Gifford

My First Football Game

"Down," he calls.
"Set," he screams.
"Hike," he strikes.
I run.
I get open.
He throws!
I catch!
I run as fast as lightning.
And…
And…
And…
Touchdown!
I score.
I do my touchdown dance.
We won!

By Justin Reid

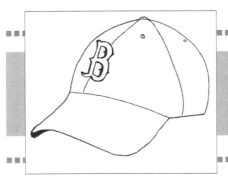

Multi-Grade Class 2–3
Ms. Jacobs

Spencer's Favorites

S ister Abby
P otato Head
E ating blueberries and ice cream
N emo Night Light
C omputer and iPad
E verything Spiderman
R ed Sox — Go Boston!

By Spencer Brenner

Noe's Favorites

N eighborhood playground and pool
O h — I love cats!
E ating chocolate chip cookies
S winging as high as the sky
G oing to Disneyland in L.A.

By Noe Scott Guzman

Will's Favorites

W ading and splashing in the pool
I nvestigating the beach
L aughing with Sophia
L ove aquariums and moon bounce
R ough housing with Dad

By Will Ross

Devon's Favorites

D irt bikes zooming outdoors
E ating pizza and fries
V ideos of *Cars* & *Toy Story*
O utside, outside, and more outside
N aming my pet rabbits Petey & Pauly

By Devon O'Donnell

Devon O'Donnell

Second Grade
Mrs. Harris

A Valley of Sunshine
Only one valley
Gets happiness every day
and sunshine to light up the day.
Only one valley gets no sadness at all,
And you can tell
They're in the valley of sunshine.
By Manmeet Singh

Ice cream
Yummy,
Good,
Delicious,
I love
Ice cream
Ice cream is creamy
There
Are
A lot
Of
Flavors
My
Favorite
Is
Vanilla
What's
Yours?
By Matthew Lauture

Dinner time
Slice!
Mash!
Potato, tomato
Boom! Crash!
Oh no!
Plates mash
Cup, spoon, knife, fork
Dinner time is going wrong!
Wait not that!
Oh no!
Dinner time a mess!
Will they like it?
What a mess!
By Josey Laughlan

My Imagination
My imagination
Is crazy and wild,
You may find flying pigs,
Exploding wigs,
And even a rich child.
You'll find teachers
Burning homework,
And my brother playing charades,
And my daddy eating
Part of a cheetah's hunted prey.
You get that it's really fun and weird,
But I have to go or else
I'll have to shave my beard.
By Aria Kimiavi

Spring

Spring is coming!
Spring is coming!
I am so glad spring is coming!
Bees and butterflies
They're all so pretty
Spring is coming!
Spring is coming!

By Kaitlyn Dougherty

Clover

A clover is a weed to us,
But a kingdom for a bee.

By Emily Marik

Lukas + Rio

One summer day
I was laying on the grass
The grass felt like an itchy cloud lifting me
My eyes were closed
A few minutes later I heard creaking
Then stomping and breathing
It started to get closer
Something slobbery was on my face
It was wet
I opened my eyes
And my dogs were pouncing and kissing
On me

By Katia Vivanco

The Pickles

Smushy, ugly, slimy
Pickles
Smushy, ugly, slimy
Gooey monsters

By Jacob Sartorius

Soccer

I like soccer.
I like how the ball
Goes right through the goal.
I like how many people
Go to a soccer game.

By Scott Howarth

Flowers

Flowers are beautiful.
Flowers are pretty.
We need flowers to live and breathe.
Flowers decorate gardens and our world.

By Sophie Strauss

My Sister

Nora,
My sister.
Special,
Nice,
Helpful.
My sister.
Cute,
Awesome,
Fun.
My sister.

By Emily Colvin

Seeds

Seeds, seeds, seeds grow big
Seeds grow gigantic quickly
Seeds turn into plants

By Robert Long

A Mountain

A mountain so marvelous
A mountain
A mountain.
A mountain so snowy
A mountain
A mountain.
A mountain so strong
A mountain
A mountain.
A mountain full of power!

By Alex Carlon

Rocks

Rocks, rocks
Everywhere
Geode
Crystal
Amethyst
And more
Turquoise
Ruby
Opal
Rocks, rocks
Every where

By Max Levy

Snow

On a cold winter night the snow came down slowly, gently, carefully.
The snow came down as quiet as a mouse
By the morning the snow had stopped.
By then there was a beautiful blanket of sparkly white snow.

By Theo Smith

Homework

Homework,
Homework,
Homework,
I need to do my homework.

The due date is tomorrow!
I finished my homework.
Oh no!
I forgot to do my math homework.

By Jackson Crawford

Trash Can

Crackady, crack
As the winds
Blow trash inside.
I throw.
I jump
To reach the
Trash can.
Trash, trashy, trash.
I put it in
With a crickle and crackle sound.
I throw a piece of foil
In the trash can.

By Aretha Williams

Butterflies

Butterflies
In the sky
Butterflies, see them fly.
Pink ones, yellow ones
See them fly by.
All the people with their butterfly hats
Sway through the grass in the summer and fall.

By Marina Jansen

Playground… Playground… Playground
Playground
Can I take a bath on the playground?
Can I do my homework on the playground?
Can I play with Matthew on the playground?
How about Oliver?
Can I play with him also?
I can play on the playground.
I love the playground because there is an awesome silver slide that you climb up and slide back down!!!!!!!
I love the playground!

By Zach Savory

Mother's Day
It's Mother's Day!
Stress.
Wake up early.
Got to zip.
Got to get mom a present.
Not just any present.
I've been through chocolate roses,
Tarts, and her favorite breakfast.
I've found the perfect present.
Spending time together.

By Emma Sebastian

Art
Drawing is very fun
And awesome.
Very cool,
Looks great!
Use color or paint.
You can draw
Anything you want
Like a flower,
Or a tree.
Anything is possible
In art.

By Oliver Giaon

The Box
A box.
I wonder what's inside?
Packing peanuts?!
Oh, yeah I forgot I ordered this box of packing peanuts.
Now I can I make a scale model of the Empire State building!
And the box is going to be an office building right next to it.
Steady… I am on the last one
Now I have to avoid knocking it down.
I'm DONE!!!
NOOO!! I destroyed it!
I wonder what I could build next…

By Chris Panatier

Flying

I	
lift	and
my	see
wings	birds
in the	flying
air what	thinking
a delightful	how I used
feeling	to
I	be
hear	bored

By Natalie Gainer

Multi-Grade Class 2–3
Ms. Bursk

Sammy

S miley
A lways says "hi"
M om's biggest fan
M oves in P.E.
Y oung gentleman

By Sammy Allred

Synthya

S inger!
Y oung lady
N ever backs down
T aps to a beat
H appy girl
Y ellow
A rm strength

By Synthya Rojas Barrera

Lakshmi

L oves techno pop music
A lways moving
K ind
S howers the room with personality
H opes for gym or library
M akes us laugh
I nterested in singing

By Lakshmi Arun

Zuhayr

Z any
U nderstands directions
H elpful
A lways happy
Y oung gentleman
R ises to the occasion

By Mohammad Zuhayr Khawaja

Third Grade
Mr. Kidder

Me and My Brother
We look alike
But we're not alike
I like ice cream
And I like candy
I like cookies
I like computers
I like Sprite
Hi-C's fine
But we have something we can both agree on…
We both like TV !

By Morgan Pew

Dinosaurs in Prehistoric Time
Big, small
They are always different types
One could fly
Another walks
And one could swim.

By Dhruv Dewan

My Dog
My dog was awesome
My dog was cool
She watched TV
And played with me too
Then she
Died
And I was
Sad

By Jess Galliher

Bey Blade
I'm doing a battle,
STORM PEGASUS vs. DARK WOLF
3, 2, 1…
Let it rip!
Attack now Pegasus!
Ting Ting
What? I lost?
Come on
Not yet!
Pegasus special move, starblast!
BOOM!
I won!

By Ahmad Rauf

School
School is fun
Math, science, reading, writing
All of it
School is fun
Recess, lunch, PE, and dismissal
School is fun!

By John Link

Stuff that Starts with "P"
For lunch I have pepperoni pizza
With purple pants
And a pink shirt on
Today I got a puppy and named him
Mr. P

By Isibeal Measells

Spring

Spring is NOT awesome.
Pollen dancing into my eyes
Itchy all over
Sneezes
Flowers bloom, it spells doom

By Daniel Koester

I Can't Go to School Today

I'm sorry mom I cannot go to school today
I feel like a horse without any hay
My throat is sore my hands are clammy
My hair is turning white, just like Granny
My eyes are red
My toes are wrinkled
My stomach hurts
My arms are crinkled
What?
It's Saturday?
Forget this I'm going out to play!

By Samantha Peters

Soccer

I'm playing an exciting game
I'm exercising
I'm running to the goal
I'm shooting the ball
I'm playing against a team
I'm losing the ball
I'm winning the game
I'm taking my penalty shot
I'm scoring my penalty shot
The ref blows time
Whistle, half time
I get some water
The ref blows the whistle again
I'm playing the second half
I'm running to the goal
I score
We win!

By Willy Burnett

Who am I?

I am fast.
I am deadly.
I have a sword.
I can blend in with the night
I can tell if you're awake
My skill cannot be matched
Who am I?

By Simon Luai

Nice Mom, Mean Kid

Mom! I need some food!
It's in the kitchen sweetie
And you're in the kitchen.
But my legs are tired!
It's right in front of you.
My arms are tired!
I need you to feed me.
You're not a baby.
Mom!

By Nicole Giery

Swimming

Fly, breast, free, back,
Swimming fast, swimming slow,
Doing flip turns
Open turns
25, 50, 100, 125
150, 200
Ribbons
Blue, red, white, and green

By Ryan Vintimilla

Tombs

Ancient pharaohs lie in tombs,
Buried with jewelry, wine, and food.
They go to the afterlife,
Where life is great.
They need a boat to get them there.

By Rachel Aguilera

Honey
There once was a bear named Honey
Everyone thought he was funny
Then he went to town
And worked as a clown
And made himself lots of money

By Meredith Wagner

Headbands
Headbands,
Shiny black,
Metallic red,
Gold with sparkles,
Silver with gems,
White with a bow.
I love headbands!

By Liz Milausnic

Penguins
Penguins are cute
And can be small.
They like to slide off the iceberg
Into the deep blue sea.
They eat little fish and shrimp.
They feed their babies with their food
The end of the day comes soon.

By Elspeth Berry

Recorder
Blow hard, blow soft,
Make notes
Make good songs
Small recorders, large recorders
Any size you want
Made out of wood or plastic
However you want
Just make sure you don't break it
Or you'll have to take it!

By Chad Nazam

Midnight
In the night it strikes midnight.
A single wolf howls
At the big curved crescent moon.
I just can't wait until the next day arrives

By Christopher Le

Cheetah
Zoom, Zoom, 75 mph
Spots, ZOOM, caught
My lunch.

By Jimmy Lowe

Helicopter
You better hang on tight
So you won't fall out
When the blades spin
It makes lots of noise
You better hang on tight boys!
So when you're on your flight
Don't have any fright.

By Austin Palik

Thrills
Ready
So so ready!
Just want to
Get out
I need need!
To have
The
Thrills!

By Antonia Rosoiu

Shadows
Shadows are everywhere
In light and darkness
You make them
Shadows

By Stephen Esse

Third Grade
Ms. Raphael

UFO

A ship is in my yard
I think it's a UFO.
I can't play outside
We called the cops,
They thought we were prank callers.
In the middle of the night
Something came out.
I woke up in a ship
And aliens were inside!
Ahhhhhhh!

By Jerome Scott

Ballet

Tap, tap, tap
In my point shoes.
Dancing like snowflakes
Glittering in the sky.
Costumes and make up.
Oh, it's time to dance-
Got to go!

By Audrey Kelley

The Pink Polar Bear

There was a bear
Who was polar.
His name was Kevin,
And he was pink.
He drank a pink drink,
And ate blue shoes.

By Rachel Smith

Athos

He's fluffy, he's messy,
He's funny, he's silly.
He's cuddly, he's sweet,
So I give him a treat.
He's hard to resist,
Easy to pick,
He makes me comfortable
When I'm sick.
He is a mess, but he isn't a hog.
But yup he's my DOG!
He needs me, I need him.
We always play outside or in.
We always have fun no matter what,
He gets jealous when I find a mutt.
He's my pup, a little of a slob,
But yup he's myDOG!

By Julia Nielsen

Apple Goes Crazy

iPhone
iPod
iPad
iPhone 4
iPod touch
iPod nano
iPod shuffle
iPod original
Does everything have
To start with *i*?

By Max DeLeon

Pink Drink

I went to the store,
I wanted a drink.
I looked on the shelf,
I saw something pink.
I opened the cap, and boy did it
STINK!
I went to the cashier,
I bought the drink.
When I got home
I thought it was a cup of lemon-lime.
I put the pink drink in the sink.
It exploded out of the sink.
And boy, did it
STINK!

By Rae Gose

Chess

Chess is awesome!
I get a draw,
A stalemate,
A checkmate.
There is a king,
and a queen,
Rooks,
Bishops,
Knights,
And pawns.
Sometimes I win,
Sometimes I lose,
And it's always fun to play.

By Cody Withers

My Fake Fever

I have a really bad fever.
I have chicken pox,
Stuffy nose, sore throat,
And a very bad cough.
I'm staying home
For three weeks.
It's so *easy*
To fool my MOM.

By Nyanne Tucker

No Bones

This person has no bones.
A bull has to drag him.
Ow!
He's laying on the rug,
Burn on his skin.
Bull has to do everything for him.
"I like this," says the man with no bones.
The bull does not,
So he leaves.
And the man with no bones,
Lays there for the rest of his life.

By Peter Sharp

Red
Red, red,
The color of blood
The color of fire trucks
The red star floating helplessly in the sea
The stripes on the flag
The new month of June

By Bryan DeLaine

My Crazy Dog!
Ramming walls,
Falling down,
Plop!
He's electric,
Pow! Pow!
Scram! Scram!

By Harvey Dietz

Frogs
Frogs love to jump
They love to swim
Something that stumps me…
Is how great they swim.

By Samantha Kosowiec

Ninja
Throwing star,
Smoke bomb,
Missions,
Spying,
Grappling hook,
Swords,
Disguised.
Darn! Captured!

By Amman Ahmad

The Olympian's Powers
Strike!
Goes Zeus' lightning bolt.
Whish!
Goes the sea.
Rumble!
Goes the Underworld.
That's the Olympian's powers.

By Jaden Logan

That Cat
That cat can be naughty,
That cat can be nice,
That cat can be *purring*,
That cat sometimes scratches me,
That cat sometimes bites me,
That cat is fat--OOOPS!
I got terribly scratched by
THAT CAT!

By Emma Rose Holtzman

Ninjas
They jump,
Whoosh!
They bump their swords, Shing!
They attack, Boom!
They jump onto a dragon,
Bam!

By Hunter Black

My Kitty Cat, Slash

Fast orange!
Fluffy, tricky!
Run, run, run!
Then he finally goes to …
Sleep.
Oh, no!
He's on the pillow again.
Get off the pillow,
It's not for you.
Finally, I find his cat toy.
I wind it.
It goes, then he goes.
Oh, no!
Another problem…
He's running again!
Slash! Slash! Slash!

By Katya Shakula

There Is a Monster Under My Bed

There is a monster under my bed.
I know it! No lie! Gulp.
What if I'm dead monster meat?
What if I make it past the night?
Hurray! I hope.

By Ethan Khoshand

Paper Airplane

ZOOM!
Breaks through the wind,
Glides so good,
Does tricks in the air,
ZOOM!
Lands smoothly.
ZOOM!

By Jack Stringer

Too Much

Too much dogs,
Too much cats,
Too much people,
Too much hats!

Too much men
Too much trash,
Too much clouds,
Too much goes crash!

Too much snow,
Too much sun,
Too much numbers,
Too much fun!

Too much paper,
Too much pens,
Too much pencils,
Too much friends!

Too much bees,
Too much birds,
Too much everything,
TOO MUCH WORDS!

By Stephanie Silverio

Electronics

PSP
PS2
PS3
I phone
I pad
I pod nano
I pod shuffle
I pod touch
Wii
3DS
DSi XL
DS light
Xbox
Boom box
Kindle
Nook
Radio
Laptop
Computer
TV
1 hour
2 hours
3 hours
STOP!

By Caden Lintner

Roller Coasters

Up and down,
All around,
See how fun it can be
To ride in circles.
Flips or glides down
To the floor.
Up again,
On another ride,
Till the day ends.

By Ariana Foronda

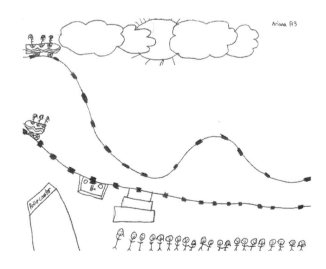

Third Grade
Ms. Robles-McCormack

Fish

Fish swim in the deep blue sea
He swims far away
At night the moon
Lights the way
At day the sun
On the way he eats food
Like seaweed and plants

He runs across a ship
Where I see him swim
He keeps swimming
He runs into a shark
This is a Great White
He swam and swam
And till safe again
Off again to sea

He goes to coral reef kingdom
Where he stays a week
Then swims again
In the deep blue sea alone
He blows some bubbles
He blows more
He is happy
He swims again
He meets a dolphin
He runs away
He is now here
He is home!

By Emma Grossback

Cheese

Cheese is deliciously delicious.
It is mostly yellow or white.
I consider it as beautiful as a rainbow.
It makes me feel wonderful
Everytime I eat cheese
I feel like I'm in another world
Cheese can be parmesian or cheddar
Cheese can be cheesy when it's cheese
CHEESE!

By Riya Unde

Plants

Plants! Plants! They are great
I love plants and you should too
Plants are a nice green

By Samanvita Kolachana

Flames

Flames are very hot
You better not touch one or
You'll get very very hot
You might even scream
So all the dimensions can hear you.
You might even die
It wouldn't be cool
If you do,
Don't blame me
I did warn you.

By Mithun Vidhya-Ponraj

Flowers

Flowers flowers in the air,
Flowers flowers everywhere.
Flowers purple, flowers blue,
I love flowers yes I do.

By Alina Ampeh

Violets

Violets are pretty
Its petals are purple
On a field of violets
Everybody wants one
Let's pick them
Ten are only left
So come on quickly!

By Aastha Mistry

Lightning

Lightning is so cool.
Lightning shocks lots of people.
Lightning is so hot

By Nikash Sawant

A World Without Colors

Could you imagine a world without colors?
You couldn't see what was what
You would only see black and white
Or worse just black
Anything and everything
You would be blind and invisible
So that's why you have to have a world with colors

By Divya Dasari

Green

Some things are blue, some things are orange, but there is one color that stands out most of all. It's the color of the grass and color of a turtle, its green of course my favorite color.

By Riley Heitmann

Snakes

Snakes are coiled around the world,
Slashing, biting, fun!
For them, at least, for us, not much.
They like basking in the sun!
They find their prey,
Sink in their teeth,
Daring not to make a mistake!
Racing through the forest-
What fun to be a snake!

By Riley Van Hilst

Basketball

Basketball is fun because
You can hit your friends on the
Head with the basketball

By Arjun Wente

Flowers

Flowers are Beautiful
Lovely as can be
Orkets are pink and white
With bee's and butterfly's flying around
Excellent Tulips everywhere
Roses are red
Sunflowers are yellow

By Celeste Constantine

Ice Cream

Ice cream ice cream
I wish I could eat it everyday.
Chocolate cup sugar cone
It wouldn't matter anyway.

By Gabrielle McClellan

Basketball

Dribble, dribble, shoot.
Go ahead and steal the ball.
Dribble, shoot, shoot, shoot.

By Cyrus Rodriguez

What Exactly Is A Flower?

What exactly is a flower?
A flower is a piece of art and each one is crafted
But exactly what is a flower?
A flower is like a gift from Mother Nature
But exactly what is a flower?
A flower is like us humans who needs stuff to
survive and live though struggles
But exactly what is a flower?
A flower is a bee's best friend

By Megan Slater

The Road Ends Here

Does the road end here?
Is there nothing else beyond this point?
Why do such roads have to be blocked
By such signs?
All of these questions cannot
Be answered by mankind
For only nature is wise enough for this.
Why! Come to think of it,
Yes it is only a sign
But what is beyond this point no one will ever
Know until someone opens their heart and
Explores beyond this place.
That someone is me

By Margarita Gamarnik

Trees, Trees, Trees

Count the trees!
Count them by threes!
Wait, to many.
Don't count the trees.

By Madelaine Cross

My Birthday Presents!!

I was sitting on the ground…
I was opening presents for hours
It feels like it!
My bottom is feeling numb
I love all the presents…
But I wish I could
Just sit in a chair and
I wish my mom could stop
taking pictures of me!
I am starting to become blind!
My foot is starting to become asleep
I wish I had a better life!

By Ashley Milligan

Baseball

Baseball is awesome
I like baseball it is fun
Baseball is so fun
By Samuel Klein

Reading

Open a door to a wonderful world
Full of myths and magic,
Learning and fun,
History and mystery,
See colorful pictures
Read blasting words
Open this door to a magical world
From so long ago
By Anna Goldman

Flowers

Violets, crocuses,
Irises, cherry blossoms, daisies, roses, sunflowers,
tulips, gardenias, jasmines
They all are so beautiful to me
They all are so nice but I can't believe the price
Flowers flowers
What should I do?
What should I do?
By Sofia Briceno

Snowflakes

Soft
Nice
Outside
Wet
Flakes
Little
Awesome
Kind of sparkles
Exciting
Silver
By Emily Ye

Oh No! Not The Cat!

EveryBuddy needs a Buddy
(that's what my owners say.)
So when you think about it
they've got it the right way.
And why I say this? Well you might guess.
The reason is:
Cats are a mess. One day I went out
on a walk but I did
not know cats liked to stalk.
But as I walked I was being stalked.
Not by a frog or another nice dog.
No of course it was worse:
it was a cat. A naughty little brat that cat it is,
it always looks for trouble.
And when in luck got double.
But not this time would there be another crime,
for I would run away on that very day.
But then the cat saw me looking like she'd
like to claw me.
And then the cat
who should be chasing a cat
instead is
chasing me!
By Alexandra Davis

Eruption

<pre>
Not   Entertaining
Really   Rough
         Unenjoyable
         Painful
         Trouble
         Intense
         Outrageous
         Not   Fun
</pre>

By Andrew Sivak

Basketball

Basketball
All
Is
Cool
Baskets
Trying
Balls
All
Low
Love

By Alexander Constantine

Life In A Pencil

You can write whatever you want
when you have a pencil
Anything you want,
fantasy, fiction, biograghy, and even poetry
But I think writing about life
is the best so far
Sometimes I even do it in the car!
You should always always
Draw a picture to go
Because then it surely wont flow
Some times I like reading
Some times I like writing
But either way I'm thinking!

By Julia Nassau

Basketball

Basketball is fun
I like basketball
Half court or full court
Basketball is fun
High baskets or low baskets
Either one is fun
I like basketball
Basketball is fun

By Samuel Joyner

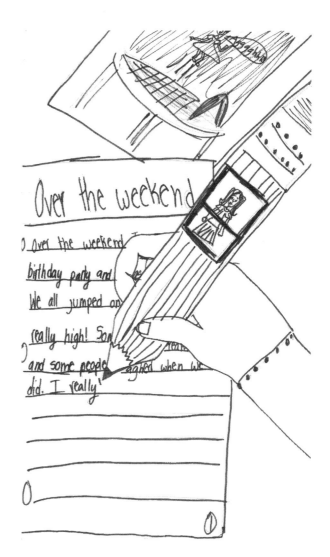

Ms. Booth

Fourth Grade

Sincerely Your Pet Rock

Dear Old Friend of Mine,
Do you remember me?
I am your pet rock
You use to be my best friend
But then you
Got a dog and forgot about me.
I've been waiting for you
Sitting out in the cold.
Will you take me inside?
I won't make a peep.
You can put me in a flower pot.
Oh I made you a poem.
Take me inside.
Take me inside.
I will give you this poem
And make you french fries.
I'm tired of the cold just take me inside.
Sincerely,
Your pet rock

By Nikki Corey

My Dad

Loving and caring
He was born in
Britain
I like the British ways
You agree mostly with what I say
You are nice
You are always my
Dad

By Gavin Leonard

Football

Football is fun
First down, second down
See your man run
Touchdown the whistle blows
The look on his face, the player knows
You're out of your seat and on your feet
An awesome score lights up the board
Field goal, extra point a better drink they've
Never poured.

By Jackson Cook

Beach

I went to the beach and
I got crushed by a wave
I came out crying then
I yelled at the wave
The wave didn`t answer
I thought it was shy.

By Alex Deeds

My Forest in the Back

My forest in the back.
Spooky, scary.
Too scary to go.
My forest in the back.
Full of monstrous creatures
The noises they make.
What would you do there?
With monstrous eyes
Staring at you.

By Mystic Worthington

Marvel

Marvel is a hero like Captain America,
Spiderman, Thor, Hulk, Ironman, Red Hulk,
Hawk guy, Antman and Ghost Rider
A hero sometimes has a number like zero.
A hero has a power
Like to fly in the air then fight a bear
A hero can fly really high.

By Michael Said

Hair & Underwear

My hair
Matches my underwear
And does not care
If I dare
that I can fly in the air
And kick
A chair
And kill a bear
Guess what my hair
Matches my
Underwear.

By Adam Sharaf

Jacob

Soft, cuddly, cute
But don't lose him because he might
Never come out.
His tail is like a bowling ball
Ready to be hit.
Soft, cuddly, cute
Jacob

By Lucy Smith

My Dog Moby

He is fun
My dog Moby
I love him

By Anton Coghlan

The Basement

Don't go to the basement
It will spookafie you.
The cold wind
B   l   o   w   i   n   g
Ear to ear
It makes you
Shiver but
T   h   a   '   s
A
WARNING
Look for yourself
BOO!

By Adam Thomas

Stealth Attack

The scaly body swiftly moves
Through the sea of sand
In search of an unlikely rodent
That will be his supper
80 feet away he smells a mouse
The slits in his eyes sharpen
He darts as fast as he can
The mouse has no idea
What hit him
Snap!!!
There goes the mouse.
He is now Snake food!!!

By Ashwin Umaselvan

Lucy B4

My Cats
One is
White
And black
Like a
Chess board
Waiting to get
Pet
The other
One is black
Like the night
Sky
Meow
Meow
Meow
Like an alarm
Clock when
You just
Wake up
By Asher Levy-Myers

TACO!
Taco you're good!
Taco you're awesome!
Taco you're cheesy!
Taco you're yummy!?
By Justin Wolcott

Alone
Alone all day
No brothers
No sisters
Sometimes
I feel sad
Because
I don't
Have a
Lad
(a.k.a friend)
A L O N E
By Julianne Holmes

Rio the Dog
Bark! Bark! Bark!
Rio is a
Basset Hound.
He is my dog.
If you feed him,
He will swallow it in one
Bite.
That's why he is so
Chubby!
Bark! Bark! Bark!
He loves people, and people
Love him.
Bark! Bark! Bark!
His eyes are very droopy,
And he acts a little loopy.
He has long lips,
And he is short.
Bark! Bark! Bark!
He runs fast
Because his speed is like
Lightning!
(For a fat dog)
By Kristine Vivanco

What If?

What if your brother said bye to his pie?
What if you were a king with brown hair, a golden crown and always wore a frown?
What if your bunny was acting funny?
What if your cat chased a rat but landed on a mat and then a bat that chats flew down and caught the rat that got stuck in the hat?
What if a parrot was eating a carrot?
What if a bee held a tree?
What if my pet rode a jet to vet and got wet?
What if I had a mate named Kate who always came in late?
What if your bell fell into a well and yelled "Look I found a shell!"

By Portia Anthony

Books

Books are
Funny and mysterious,
Strange and real, weird and dumb,
Fake and entertaining, interesting and suspense
Exciting and different, sad and stupid
Confusing and amazing.
Those are the reasons why I like books.
Books are awesome.

By Kian Elliott

Fire Alarm

RING RING !
Class single file line
RING RING !
Class out to the grass
RING RING !
Class face forwards
RING RING !
Class quiet
RING RING !
Class start walking
RING RING !
Class stop walking
Silence
Class go back to the classroom…
RING RING !
NOT AGAIN !

By Nicolle Hendzel

Snow Day

One morning I looked out the window
And saw a white, powdery substance
S l o w l y
D
R
I
F
T
I
N
G
Towards the ground.
My first thought is yeah, snow day.
No school!
But in a second
I find myself on my bed
And I realize that I was dreaming.
So I start waiting
Waiting for a snow day.

By Farris Ahmad

Joey

Lazy
Knows three tricks
Sit, paw,
And
Sleep
We think (our family)
Thinks he's part cat
because he likes to
eat a lot of cat food
and cat food and
cat food.

By Calvin Warstler

The Mystery Animal

It can be white as can be
It can be brown like a tree
It can be gray in a scene
What is it? Can you guess?
A rabbit
A snow fox
A bear
A squirrel

By Matthew Dim

The Telly

(P.S must speak this in British)
Mother handed over me the remote
"I'm going to watch the telly"
I said and-I-quote
I turned on the telly
And CNN news was on
"This is totally ridicules"
I said to my mom
Then I turned on Sponge Bob
The show that rules
This is totally better
Than that doo doo.

By Olivia Nielsen

Mermaids

Mermaids,
swimming silently through the ocean.
Perched on jagged rocks,
singing sweetly.
With necklaces of pearl,
tails glittering
like
a
rainbow.
Diving through
underwater
caves,
exploring.
Gliding
with
fish
and dolphins.

By Miranda Sandoval

Fourth Grade
Mrs. Crisafi

Dog Did It!
Ate my homework
My dog did it
Tracked mud in the house
My dog did it
Had a accident
My dog did it
Hurt the baby
My dog did it
Tracked paint on the floor
Uhhhhhhhhhhhhhh

By Trey Rachal

Drum
New
Shiny
Drum

Bong
Bong
Bong

Delightful sounds
Fill the
Air
Bong
Bong
Bong
Old broken drum

By Jackson France

The Dive
As I run across the board
I feel a grip as strong as can be
I use the board as a springboard
To jump
In the air
As I land in to the water
I get a shiver down my spine
As the silky water goes through my hair
And through
And I LOVE it

By Filip Stanisavljev

Evil Santa
Santa steals toys from target at night
Santa breaks into our homes.
Santa captures elves and makes them his slaves
Santa hates garden gnomes. (Because he thinks
they are insulting)
Santa isn't as nice as you think
Santa is secretly mean.
Santa is only fat because
He eats too many beans.

By Michael Pieruccini

Fall's leaves

Fall's leaves,
Falling down,
In the sun,
Never done,
Falling fast,
Falling slow,
Falling multicolor whoa!

Fall's leaves,
Coloring trees,
But then falling down,
They color trees,
With many leaves,
But please do not fall down.

Fall's leaves,
I said please!
But they all fell down.
Now what am I supposed to do,
With this color shower?
I Know!

By Carla Nicolini

Tall

Tall
Bent
Out of shape

Branches
Leaves
Bark

Paper
Pencil
Planks

Tree

By Luke Dobrovic

Flute

Shiny new
Reflective
High pitched
Keys
Keyholes

Toot
Toot
Toot

Dark
Dusty
Black

Toot
Toot
Toot

By Joshua Pan

Gold Fish

I have an eye.
I have a mouth
I don't have hair
And I have flavor
I like myself in cheese flavor
I have some salt on me!
I am yellow but I am sometimes rainbow
I can't swim but I am a fish
I am DELLICOUS, but...
I am always DEAD
I am not in a fish bowl
But I am in a snack bowl
I am not in a small aquarium
I am just in a small stomach
I am not a card game
I get eaten by living creatures!!
I wish I was not a snack

By Kisaki Fukahori

I Hate My Cat

I hate my cat
He ate my fish
I hate my cat
He scratched up my guitar
He ate my fish
I hate my cat
He bit my finger
He scratched up my guitar
He ate my fish
I hate my cat
He pounced on my friend,
and then he stopped being my friend
He bit my finger
He scratched up my guitar
He ate my fish
He pounced on my friend,
and then he stopped being my friend
He bit my finger
He scratched up my guitar
He ate my fish
My cat is for sale

By James Frucht

Maggie

Makes you run for your life
(Trying to "hug" you)
Always making crafts
Gets on my nerves
Goes with mom
I play with her (sometimes)
Errors in speech

By Jack Thomas

Mom and Dad

My cousins are cool
My brother and sister are neat
And my grandparents give treats!!!
But I'll tell you one thing and one thing only
You Mom and Dad are the Best!

By Ben Harris

My Brother

My brother is nice
He is very, very funny
He always has a smile on his face
He loves LEGO's!
SOMETIMES my brother annoys me
We fight occasionally
But that's what brothers and sisters do!
No matter what he does I will ALWAYS love
Him

By Mia Giaon

That Big Red Tree

I sit under that big red tree
She just sits there smiling at me.
She lets me sit on her limbs
When I'm around her I'm never grim.
She just sits there smiling at me
Oh I love that big red tree.

By Carson Miller

Playing hockey

Playing hockey is fun,
Passing the puck,
Skating with the puck,
Shooting the puck,
Watching hockey on TV.
Working as a team, playing against my friends.
SCORE!!!!! 1-0. I love to play hockey!

By Steven Song

Red Tree

Big tree small tree
I like all the trees that be
purple, yellow, blue, and green
but my favorite is that big red tree
it just sits there talking to me
she plays with me
oh I love that big red tree

By Erin Reilly

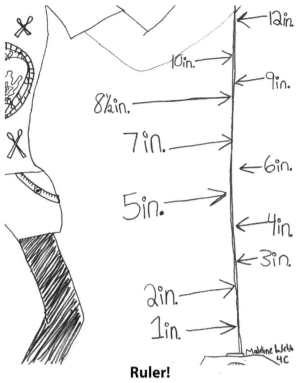

Snowmen
When I get off the bus,
The first thing I see
Are a million billion snowmen
Staring at me.
A ton of ugly snowmen
Watch me every day
They really creep me out,
I wish they'd go away.
Today I'm really happy
My wish actually came true
When I looked at the snowmen
They had melted into goo.
By Minwu Kim

Ruler!
One inch
Two inches
Ten inches
Fourteen inches
Twenty-three inches
Thirty-eight inches
Forty-four inches
Forty-eight inches
Fifty inches
ALMOST THERE !
Fifty-three inches
SO CLOSE!
Fifty-Eight!!!!!!!!!!!!!!!
I am Fifty-eight inches tall!
By Madeline Webb

The Moon
As I look up
In the sky
I see a big
White
Shining ball
Of light
I think
It's the moon
The moon sparkles
In the night sky
Oh how I love
The moon
By Caroline McBride

Snowflake
As delicate as a Feather
As heavy as Paper
If you touch it, it Melts
That's a Snowflake.
By Sophia Liao

Thoughts
Thoughts are things you think of,
And you think of thoughts.
Everything started out with thoughts,
And thoughts started everything.
My thoughts my inventions and buildings,
And my inventions and buildings
Started as thoughts.
See what you can do with thoughts,
Maybe even things that have never been done!
By Alexandra S. Habibi

Wear Green Or Else

On Saint Patrick's Day please wear green
If you don't you are mean. I guess
I'm miss judging but I swear I went to my
Friends house he said he was wearing green Underwear. I believed him his grandmother
Did not. She grabbed the waist band of his
shorts and hanged him there. I closed my eyes
His sister looked she said they were blue with
Red fish hooks! Now you see you should wear
Green or your underwear will be seen.

By Alex Ainspan

My Dog Ivan

My dog is…
Crazy
Not trusted around chocolate
Silly
And soft

He gives…
Licks on the face
And whines (when it's time to walk)

He loves to…
Beg for food
And get scraps

By Margaret Vicheck

Tree

Old and wrinkled
Tall and straight
Crooked and bent
The Tree has delicate blossoms
The Tree has fresh green leaves
The Tree sheds a beautiful color shower
The Tree is pale white
CHOP
The Tree is gone

By Michelle Yue

Winter Forest

Winter forest snow and White
Winter forest big and bright
There is a bear that sleeps all night
It's a winter forest all day and all night

By Spencer Harris

Lost dog

'He's gone!' I yelled
"He's gone!' the reply came
My favorite dog
My best companion
'He's gone' the words that echo clearly
He's gone. Without a trace
That happy bark
The fuzzy blanket
That used to be my loyal helper
Now he's gone
And I can't help it
Please, have you seen my lost dog?

By Sarah Palmer

Fourth Grade
Mrs. Gualtieri

Bacon
Thank you so much
for there are pigs in the world
Their meat is so good that
the tastes are all blurred
I think about pigs
Who have been eaten this week
too bad for the pigs 'cause they are so weak
bacon is yummy, it's awesome to eat
too bad for vegetarians because it is meat.

By Victoria Kartseva

Bob's Donuts
Bob works in a donut shop
He works behind the counter
He works all day from 7:00 am to 8:00 pm
Selling donuts to customers
One day Jack came in and asked for a dozen donuts
7 chocolate, 4 Boston cream and 1 jelly filled
Bob likes donuts.

By Adam McCormick

Breakfast
Sausage, egg, and muffins too…
I like cereal with a spoon.
Pancake, waffles and scrambled eggs…
Wish I could choose from this buffet.
Bananas and peaches-with strawberry yogurt…
I think I'm ready for dessert!

By Sierra Shuman

Bunnies
The fifth of May,
Was the day I went out to play
And before I left, my mom had said, "Don`t go far away".
So I stayed, with the trees, and under one I saw,
Not a kart, not a key.
Not some pancakes, not a pea.
But another bunny rabbit, just like me!
I went up, and I said "hi", I said "bye", I said this and that.
But the bunny was motionless, under the tree where it sat.
I went up to my mom (who was chopping up plums)
And told her about the bunny
And do you know what she told me?
That that bunny rabbit was a toy, for little girls and boys!

By Phoebe Liu

Horses
Horses are graceful and beautiful,
They are fast but sometimes slow,
They are intelligent and also understanding,
They are wild, but sometimes not,
They are friendly, but can bite,
They are clean, but mostly dirty,
Look at all the information,
My mind is going to have a transformation!

By Anna Verevkina

Chickadee de

Chick a de de
Look at me me
In the tree tree
Can you see see
Way up high high
In the sky sky
Sky as blue blue
Sunny day too
Want to play play
Hide and seek seek
Do not peak peak
Here me sing sing
Also ring ring
Chick a de de
Look at me me!

By Ankita Kalkar

Dragon Moon

One
On the mountain side
Waterfalls, drinking moonlight
The dragon climbs up
Two
The mountains up top
Up he climbs never stopping
Ice, snow, moon, light,
Three
More go up, up
One comes down seasons pass
And the third is last

By Raphael Chambers

Dragons

Soaring through the big blue sky
It's very rare to see them fly
Hotter than lava, they breathe fire
If I'm wrong, then call me a liar
Claws, wings, and spiked tail too
They fly in the in sky blue

By Alex Shen

Rainy days

Rain goes
F   D
A   O
L   W
L   N
I
N
G
To Earth making people wet
The frogs came out and
Jump in the puddles
Out comes the rainbow
ROY.G.BIV red, orange,
Yellow, green, blue, indigo and violet
This is what rainy days are made of.

By Zach Bell

My Birthday

My birthday was last year it was this year too
I invited all my family and friends too
We played games and ate cake
It is present time I'm having fun
Look what I got it is an I-touch mum
Let's go outside and play tag let's run
It is time to leave the party has come to an end
Thank you friend's for coming it would not be a party without you

By Ritika Shrivastav

That dog

That dog is rude,
It burps,
It barks,
And eats like a pig.
It smells like mud,
That was dried from the sun,
That dog never takes a bath,
It just sits there with mud,
That dog eats everything,
He eats the pillows,
My mom is going to kill me,
It eats paper,
Glue,
Everything,
He also ate my hair,
He's eating it right now
That dog.

By Clarisse Cubas-Lopez

Goal

I get on the field
I'm the fiercest girl out there
I'm lightning fast I steal the ball
Were undefeated!
We **WIN**!
We **TIE**!
We never **LOSE**
I make cuts I make passes
I head it into the **GOAL**
I dribble and cut the corner I shoot
It's a **GOAL**
No one wants to get in my way
I score a **GOAL** every game
We win every game
Every year we win the championships
Every year we each score a **GOAL**
Guess who I am …
I'm a soccer player.

By Sejal Gude

DUCKYS!

Really like duckys.
Yeah I really like duckys.
They are very cute.

They live by the lake.

Rubber ducky's look like them.

But they are rubber.

By John Carney

I'm Lost in the Circus

The circus is where you scream and shout,
Where all the animals and clowns come out,
Buy yourself some candy and more,
Then find the opening to enter…
Which door?
Oh no I'm lost,
What should I do?
I'll find a map,
That's the answer woohoo,
Hey what's that on the ground?
Half of a map is what I found,
Where could the other half be I wonder?
Hmmm,
Maybe this opening,
It's where I assume,
I walk in the tent,
And what I see?
My mother and father,
Waving at me!

By Maggie Tran

Football Failure

The quarterback said "hike"
And I ran down the field
And the cornerback tripped on the way
The safety came in
While I looked up and saw
The ball had been thrown where I stay
I made some adjustments
Got ready to jump
And jumped higher than I ever had
The ball got closer and closer and closer and then…….
It actually turned out pretty bad

By Jaden Gunn

The Addictions of Digital Gaming

Video games, video games
Burning your eyes out
Sitting, sitting
Sitting on the couch,
Just one more level,
Or two, or three
I'm almost at the boss,
So stop bugging me.

By Devon Gildea

Mischievous planets

Mischievous plants,
Mischievous planets,
Mischievous planets,
The sun and the earth,
They raised a commotion,
A commotion I tell you,
Of who should wear the shades
The earth said "NO SHADES!"
The sun was offended,
And cried "YES SHADES!",
And that raised an up
Uproar!

By Caitlin Moore

Mushroom Giants

My neighbors planted a rose and
watered it with a hose
When they slept at night
They woke up with a fright
What did they see in their garden?
Not a key, not a bee
Not their rose
But giant mushrooms!
Not ordinary mushrooms
Ones that were five times bigger!

By Ananya Vavilala

My Imaginary World

In my imaginary world
There'd be trees made of candy
And bushes of pie,
There'd be all of my friends there
And we could all fly,
We'd fly over the treetops
And the people would stare,
There'd be cookies and brownies
And pie everywhere,
The sun would shine brighter than ever before,
Because life would be perfect,
In my imaginary world.

By Maeve Keck

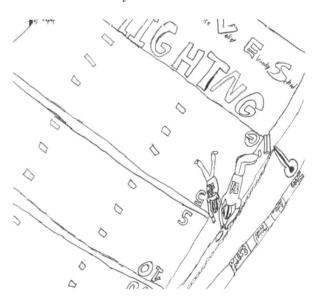

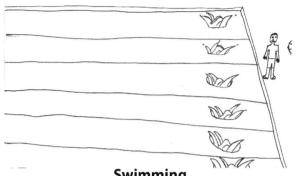

Swimming
It's early morning.
It's cold.
They call your heat.
You're waiting for the signal.
On your mark, get set, beep.
You dive in the pool.
It's really cold.
You see you're hanging behind you get in front.
Your opponent gets ahead.
Everybody is behind.
You do a flip turn.
You get ahead again.
You stay ahead.
He's gaining on you.
The wall is up ahead.
You swim as fast as you can.
You touch the wall.
You ask "who won"?
Everybody says you did.
You shake hands and then you celebrate your victory.

By Misha Podshivalov

Dragons
Dragons are so awesome with power.
They wouldn't hurt a flower.
Except they're big.
He won't eat a fig.
Dragons aren't so awesome
ANYMORE!

By Michael Encinas

The Bug
There never was a bug as snug as that bug,
All snug as a pug in a rug.
The bug was so snug it moved out of the rug,
And settled inside the mug.
A pug took the bug from its really snug mug,
And the bug was put in a jug.
He was happy 'cause the pug put him in the jug,
So he gave the pug a hug.
The pug used to be sad,
But after the hug he was glad.

By Mina Kim

The Sounds of Christmas
At my house
You can tell that it's
Christmas if you hear….
Oven timers dinging,
Cars pulling up,
Presents being opened,
Candy being eaten and the sweet whistle of my choo-choo train.

By John Carr

It's Raining Food Outside
It's raining food I run outside
My mouth is open really wide
I eat some chicken and even veggies too
Also ice cream while I scream
For its raining food outside.

By Ryan Ferzoco

Lightning
Lightning
One small crack from the sky
A crack, small but powered
A power filled with electrifying moments
Chasing each other like heartbeats:
This is lightning.

By Jeffrey Mouritzen

Fourth Grade
Mrs. Soliday

A Day at the Park
There once was a kid sitting in the park and
along came a man, it was tony stark!
Then Tony stark started to shriek, which sounded like an eagle from the highest peak.
Then a portal opened all swirly and round, and
out of the portal came a pink bloodhound.
The pink bloodhound hatched an egg, and out
came a dolphin named Greg.
Greg ate the kid and spit him out, but then his
legs formed into trouts!
But suddenly, he woke up in the park, "Thank
heavens."He said."No Tony stark."

By Cody Wright

My Carousel
I ride an hour
And then an hour back
In between the music plays
The sound in my mind
Goes around and around
Like a carousel on a track
Like me in the ring
Half-note, whole-note, sharp, or flat
Look up there goes Fox the cat
Up and down we get the beat
Up and Down the music scale
Around and around and around the trail
Glory, Regal, and especially Comet
Words on a page like a sonnet

By Sydney Cook

Homework
Homework,
Homework,
Oh why do
We need
You?
You take
Up the day
And you're
Just
No fun!!
I
Just want
To quit
School
Because of
You!
Homework
Why do we
Need
Homework?

By Kasey Corey

Pie
My family is like pie.
My mom is the cream
Smooth and fluffy and smooth.
My dad is the crust strong and hard.
My sister is the fruit soft and excited
And I'm the plate holding my family with love.

By Nathan Ide

Cupcakes

Mix the batter
Until a deep
Red.
As you
Fill the
Mixture
Into the cupcake
Pan,
Try and think
About how they
Will taste.
Then put them
Into the oven,
Take the delicious
Cupcakes out of
The oven as
Soon as you
Can smell
The red velvet
Dough
Place the
Cream cheese
Frosting smoothly
On the squishy dough.
The sadness as
I look down
At the crumbs
On my
Plate.

By Sophia Rzonca

I can't think of a poem!

I can't think of another poem!
My brain is full of foam
My paper is blank.
I want to cry!
Like a little French fry
Oh Mercy
I'm in New Jersey!

By Sai Gajula

Monkeys

Monkeys like bananas and berries
They like to
S
  W
    I
      N
        G
And go completely nuts.
That's why their my favorite animal.

By Jacob Hataway

What 6 Graders Do

They…
Build a money
Fight a shower and
climb up the Eifel Tower

By Peter Steidler

ALiENS

Invaders from Outer Space
invade the Earth with pain
no-one knows what planet
they came from.
Mercury, Venus, Mars,
Jupiter, Saturn, Neptune.
Where do they come from?

By Michael Willmore

Paranormal

Darkness falls across
The land
The
Midnight hour
Is
Closed
Again.
Step by step
Every night.

By Josh Reid

Fall

The leafs come down
One
By one.
I run to catch a leaf
If I do I'll get good luck
So I run I
F
A
L
L
But fall will catch me.
The wind dances around me.
I fall but fall will catch
Me.

By Kellie McCrea

My Dog Magic

My dog Magic
My dog Magi
My dog Mag
My dog Ma
My dog M
My dog
My do
My d
My
M

By Jesse Gleason

Cupcakes

Tasty
Fresh
Right out of the oven
Sprinkles
Frosting
Fun
Cute
Its mine
And
No one
Touches
It
Love it
Beautiful

By Ana Bradic

I'm So Bored

I'm so bored.
I'm the most bored person in the world.
I'm so bored it's just like staring at a wall.
Why can't I just chuck a ball.

By Brendan Burke

Wolves

I hear them howling every
Night
Their howls put me to
Sleep
Their fur could be a
Pillow
Oh mom a wolf would mean
A lot

By Chloe Khoshand

Rain

Drops from the Sky in water form
Then hits the ground
And disappears.

By Adam Drain

Babies

Baby 1: Hi!
Baby 2: Hi!
Baby 1: Are you a boy or a girl?
Baby 2: You think I know?
Baby 1: Whatever, I don't want to fight about it.
Baby 2: Why? You scared?
Baby 1: yes. See, if you're a boy you will beat me up, do you think I want to lose a tooth on the first day of my life?
Baby 2: what's a tooth?
Baby 1: Don't ask me.
Baby 2: so, why might I be a boy?
Baby 1: Do you like video games?
Baby 2: Yeah!
Baby 1: See, that means you're a boy and I'm a girl
Baby 2: Look, the guy to change our diapers!
Baby 1: Finally!
Baby 2: I guess you're right!
Girls can't wait and boys can!
Baby 1: Yeah!

By Jon Lister

What If

What if it's going to be the end of the world?
What if I am a robot?
What if the earth will crash to the sun?
What if Luke sky walker is my brother?
What if I will explode?
What if 2012 will happen?
What if Elmo knows where I live?
What if the cookie monster eats my cookies?
What if the Revolutionary
War starts all over again?
What if I am not good at anything?
What if I hate pie?
What if I hate candy?
What if I like math?
What if I am a girl?

By Jet Mounkhaty

Homework

Oh!
I'm sick of homework
Too much to do
I can't think
of what to do!
Shall I write a Poem
Or shall I read
Oh!
What did you say?
Today is Saturday!
Goodbye

By Jessica Din

I can't sleep

Mom I can't sleep
Why?
There's a talking truck
Jumping toy, a spider
A toy cat going meow
GO TO SLEEP!

By Delaney Duchak

The Owl Howls

The owl howls around the lake.
The owl howls at your face
The owl howls at the cowered
The owl howls in the shower
The owl howls at movies
The owl howls at smoothies
The owl howls in the air
The owl howls everywhere.

By Siraj Khatib

Books

Go to the library
pick me out a book
but I just have one request
make the author be the best

By Emily Fritz

Lego

Lego, Lego, Lego!
I love Lego's Lego
Lego Lego I can't
Stop saying it
Man I love LEGOS.
I wish I could
Never stop saying
Legos so much!

By Matthias Hammond

My To Do List

My to do list says to:
Go to a southwestern Cambodian
river which has an
under water garlic roller
coaster with a
monkey who's riding it
while trying to
eat mini purple oranges…
Then it says to:
watch a yellow owl
eat a red
monkey with
blue teeth that's
scratching an
elephants ears in
Madagascar….
Then it says:
Well, you get the picture
Love, Mom

By Cooper Spray

Monkeys

Monkeys Monkeys they like bananas.
Monkeys Monkeys they swing on vines
Monkeys Monkeys they eat more bananas
Monkeys Monkeys they pick fleas.
Monkeys Monkeys they still eat
More bananas.

By Jeremiah Noser-Munoz

Oh Homework

Homework oh homework
You stink so bad
I have to clear the room.
Oh homework, Oh homework
You kill our trees that is our oxygen
And that's why I can't believe there is
Homework, so stop the madness.

By Alex Seamans

Sunday Morning

I wake up, I can just taste it
The bacon sizzling
On the stove
Smelling the cool damp
Air of the shower gets me up
The cage of my blanket
Traps me in until
I wiggle my way out
It feels like I'm
Walking on ice when I
Take my first step on
The cold wood floor
The tip-Tap of the Faucet
Made me Thirsty
The sight of my reflection
Made me jump
YICK
Brushing needed
BADLY!!!

By Olivia Hathaway

Mrs. Giovanini

Fifth Grade

Screen Door
I opened the screen door
And sit motionless
To witness
The beauty of the night
Picturesque
The stars are twinkling
Hypnotic
Serenely quiet
All I can hear is
The rustling of the leaves
Doze off
To sleep…
By Ruma Jadhav

Autumn Leaves
In the forest filled
With autumn leaves
A dragon sleeps
Causing the leaves
To burn into smoke
With its fiery breath
By Richard Zhang

Black Birds
Black birds
Were white as snow
Until there tail feathers
Touched ink
By Sydney Haywood

The Unspoken
If darkness was bright
And mean was nice
Would the world be upside down?
If happy was sad
And normal was mad
Would the world be upside down?
If colors weren't bright
And blackness was light
Would the world be upside down?
If death was life
And wrong was right
Would the world be upside down?
Is it a question if it doesn't have an answer?
By Ambika Minocha

Things Not Seen
Here today
When you reach me
No talking
Twilight
Midnight magic
Things not seen
The eyes
Ghost cats
Long shadows
The jade stone
Ever lost
Things not seen
By Talia Makarov

Escaping

Hurry
Let's abandon
The darkness
Of that place
Hitchhike
Run into
The woods
Vanish

By Sam Simon

Rules

Travel far pay no fare
Only a witch can fly
Don't let the pigeon drive the bus

By Stephen Carey

Boom!

Boom!
The soccer ball flies through the air
Towards the guarded goal
The ball moves faster and faster
At the poised keeper
The ball heads
Right at the top corner
The goalie dives
And it's a…

By Natty Abrahams

Waffles

Waffles are a most delicious treat
With syrup that can get stuck
Onto your feet
There's also butter
Which is spread onto the crust
Enjoy the sweet smell
Wafting through the air
Waffles are usually breakfast
But lunch and dinner will always do!

By Ian Hughes

Fear

The disguise master
Speaks in tongues
Erupts into flames of doubt
Slinks slyly
To play upon the most vulnerable
Fear shuns the strong
Fear will make you mad
Change yourself
So beware
As you drift
In the current of fear
The journey
Out will be hard
And you may be scared
By the rocks by the river
Of fear

By Emily McGrath

Stinkbugs

Maggie has a bug in her hair
And hasn't noticed yet!
It's creeping up and down and
EEW! It's crawling down her neck!
But Maggie's sleeping, sleeping, sleeping
It is creeping, creeping, creeping
WE ARE SCREAMING, SCREAMING, SCREAMING
Maggie is STILL sleeping!

By Jessie Yu

Magic Moon Light

The sky is dark
The moon is bright
The sand between my toes
The ocean's waves
Washing the shore
The night is still
The moment is magic
Walking on an endless beach

By Anna Liang

Robin

Flying high
Over our head.
Chirping like a flute.
Builds a nest up in a tree.
Robin sings a song.
Searching for worms
For her chicks.
They'll grow up to be strong.
Throughout spring
And summer too.
I feed you seeds and bread.
Then fall comes around
And you take your family south.
Then next spring
You come back
In a flowery world
To sing and dance some more.
By Lily Vogel

My Fish

When I was five
I got a fish
I got pretty purple pebbles
For the bottom of its dish

I fed it every day
I named it goldired
And cleaned his bowl too
A week later it was dead
By Gwyneth Pudner

Cake

A soft creamy island,
That you can eat.
A sweet smell wafting and swirling
Around you.
I can almost taste it,
One small bite and
It fills my mouth with sweetness.
By LiPin Wang

I Am

I am
The conch bearer,
Public enemy #2,
The dragon heir,
Vanishing boy,
The magic thief,
Gregor the overlander,
The ranger's apprentice,
I am
Your imagination
By Zaahir Santhanam

Shooting the Moon

Shooting the Moon
What a Great Idea!
Falling Up
Halfway to the Sky
Cloud Land
By Maggie Klein

Goal

I feel the ball touch my cleat
I fake right, and then go left
I feel the defender nudge me
As I pass by him
I have the goal in sight
Running in the open
I feel the cool
Wind brushing through my short hair
I hear the coaches
Instructing their teams
I hear the parents cheering
I pass to my teammate
And then run to get open
Then, once again
I have the ball at my feet
While charging forward with the ball
I dribble past my defender
I swing my leg back
And shoot
I watch the ball flying
Through the air
And the next thing I hear
Is my favorite sound
The ball hitting the net
GOAAAAAALL!!!!!

By Bardia Kimiavi

World Cup

Running through the crowds,
Feeling the anxiety,
Wondering if you're going to
Make it on time,
Speeding through security
And lines of people,
Blowing your Vuvuzuela
As loud as you can,
Watching the players
Warm up,
Hearing the national anthems
Of each team
Crystal clear in your ear,
Watching the referee blow the whistle
That signals the
Start of the game,
Watching camera's
Flash like stars
In a dark night,
Yelling and
Shouting
When your favorite team scores,
Running to catch the shuttle bus,
Reliving the game
In your mind

By Karim Yafi

Baseball

Baseball is really fun
When you play it
Or watch a
Major league game
While at the stadium
You'll smell the concessions
And see the players
And the excitement
Will rush through you
If you show up early
You get to meet the players
But first you should get
Season tickets
There are also 30 teams
Over 300 Hall of Famers
Hundreds of records
And thousands of superstars
When I was three
My family got Orioles season tickets
And that was when they were good
You'll hear fans screaming
And the crack of the bat
But the most exciting thing
Is being the player
Who gets honored

By Danny Mercuri

A Saltwater Blanket

When I step inside the ocean,
I get a shiver from the cold water,
As if I had stepped into a deep
Pile of snow.
I go deeper in the water,
A giant wave is forming.
The wave is like a tall wall of water,
Piling above me.
The wall curves,
And wraps me around
In a saltwater blanket.

By Mimi Drozdetski

Stealing the Moon

I climb up the branches
Of my tree
No ladder needed
It's just me.
I climb up to the top
Reach up,
And bring it down.
One of earth's
Treasures.
I
Stole
The
MOON

By Giovanna Moriarty

A World to Remember

The world is silent,
All is still,
The world war ends, world peace comes,
Opposite forces of nature,
Join together like yin & yang,
This is the world I want to live in.

By Brianna Aguilera

Things Not Seen

Things Not Seen
The Music of Dolphins
Words of Stone
Strange Happenings
Midnight Magic
River Secrets
All the Lovely Bad Ones
Things Not Seen
Anything But Typical

By Surosree Chaudhuri

When Fire Alarms Go Mad

When fire alarms go mad,
They run around the school,
When fire alarms go mad,
They shriek and yell too,
When fire alarms go mad,
They break the golden rule,
When fire alarms go mad,
I'd know,
Because there's one in our school!

By Cal Kopstein

One Chance

The final warning
Wheel wizards basketball
Battle last shot
Weaving the rainbow
LUCKY

By Druv Sardana

Slurpee Attack

I go to get a slurpee
After a hard day's work
I slurp it into my dry mouth
A blast of cherry flavor
Tingles my tongue
I suck up a gigantic slurp and
Uh Oh!
BRAIN FREEZE!!!

By Grace Fisher

Gnats

They swoop and swarm through the air,
Disappearing into your eyes
And in your ears,
Nothing can get in their path,
I wish they would vanish out of thin air
And stop interrupting my concentration
When I'm outside.

By Devin Furness

Books

Books books books read reading
Books books books books
Books are a place to escape to books words
Swirling around in my head
Books reading reading
Books books books books books
Books painting a picture in my mind
Books a picture of stars
Books books books books reading
Books books books
Books words coming together to
Make a story book
Book read books books books
Books books books books

By Madison Flammang

Yellow Banana

Riding
Under the sun
On the clear blue water
Swaying
From
Side
To
Side
Bobbing
Up
And
Down
Yellow banana
How do you stay afloat?

By Michael Gamarnik

Fifth Grade
Mr. Huffer

Mean Monkey
I was walking through NASA station
I bought a balloon
There was a
Mean
Mad
Monkey
That was supposed to go to the moon
But
Instead
He came up to me
Poked me in the eye
With his thumb
He threw my balloon into the
Air
And it went up
Forever

By Griffin Scanlan

The Thing
Here it is
The nicest, best looking and fastest
Thing I have ever seen
Took it for a spin
Here I am covered in dirt
And excitement
I stand on a hill and yell
I have the nicest good looking
Bike in the
WORLD

By Peter Burnett

The Hungry Mouse
The mouse scattered
Through the house
Cheese please
He thought to himself
As the rain drizzled outside
Everything was silent
Not even a squeak
For the mouse was asleep

By Isabel Laxton

The Night
The night was dark
The roof was shaking
I was scared
The clock struck
It was midnight
A hurricane was out

By Trinity Gamble

Riding on a Horse
I was riding down a hill on my horse
First he was walking
Then he was trotting
Then I didn't even know it
But he was galloping
I felt like I was going to fall off
Then he started jumping
It was scary but really fun
That was the first time I ever jumped a horse

By Kelsey McLain

Aquarium

I wake up in my new home
All my friends are still asleep
I explore my home
It looks the same
I try to swim out
But …
I hit something
Something I couldn't see
And something starts staring at me
Something I've never seen
It stares at me with interest
My friends hide with fear
But I'm interested and stay
I'm at a place called an aquarium
And I love it

By Katie Vintimilla

Horseback Riding

As I ride through the forest,
On my horse Danny Boy I feel free
I'm happier than any other kid in the world.
Trees whisper
Leaves crackle under Danny Boy's hooves
He trots down the hills
I know he feels free like I do.

By Cameron Cruz

Dying in the Garden

The gate and the butterfly rust together
They are so near yet so far
Here they are
One another
Dying in the garden
And they're dying at night
Scared to death
In your heart you cry
As your garden dies
Goodbye

By Domonique Thorne

San Francisco

The wind tosses my hair
And for a split second
I become part of the wind

I look down the giant rolling hills
That are black with asphalt
And crammed on either side with houses
Perfectly lined up like books on a shelf

The clouds only seem an arm's length away
I stand atop a hill
Higher that all the rest

Just through a winding, woody path
Stands Coit tower
Tall and proud
At the top, the very top

Then I will be able to look down and see
The ocean with its boats outlining the horizon
The cars that will look like ants
I know I should be going

But I,
I savor the moment
So I can hold it in my heart forever

By Jacqueline Dubois

Dart Monkey
I was at my cousin's party
When a monkey jabbed me with its thumb
Then threw a dart at my balloon
My balloon popped
It was lost forever

By Adam Gulakowski

Lost
I am on a camping trip.
I walk
In the woods.
Help!
I am lost.
I devour my last sandwich,
Then I eat only snow.
I come to a prairie
I see a man
Walking,
And I am
Saved!

By Christopher John Yon

Eagle
I am the eagle
Soaring
Dipping
Diving
Over mountains
Lakes
And plains
As I soar I feel strong
Like I own everything I can see
I feel light as a feather
Floating in the wind
As powerful as a hurricane
I once flew through

By Lauren McCormick

Hurricane
A Hurricane.
Spins
Through the night.
Brings danger
Wood splinters
Houses crack,
Crash into the street
People scream
In the village.

By Michael Pekar Jouanneau

Right There!
There,
Right there!
Right on the rug!
Could that be a little bug?
Maybe it came from the basement.
Or from a treasure box.
Maybe even from a chicken
With chicken pox.
So now do you see there?
Oh, wait a minute,
It's just a ball of hair.

By Ian Cobb

Be the Best You Can

So intense
Try to win the NBA series
Game seven
The second you get the ball
Your heart starts bumping
You have to get the
Ball in the basket
5,4,3,2 1 swoosh
Eeeeeeeeeee!
3 points
Crowd goes wild
Ahhhhhhhhh!!!!!!!!!!!

By Zack Ahmad

Drowning

My feet sit dangling in the water
Someone pushes me
Suddenly water surrounds my body
I try to scream
Nothing
Slowly I start to sink
Trapped
Franticly pushing
Kicking
Strong arms pull me up
Breathing
Panting
Saved

By Nehal Jain

Toy Plane

I wound up the propeller
I thought of it flying
Ben let go, whoosh
It sailed
I was excited
It fell
It hit the mulch
33 feet

By Jacques Brown

Survivor

Taking in the room that survived
I looked through the blinds
Seeing
I saw a deep inviting purple object
Floating
Floating in the dark mud
Just outside of the only room
The room
The one that survived
A flower all alone
Silently
I picked up my pen
Drawing the only flower right in the center of
my notebook
It was a symbol
A memory
The memory of all that was lost
And me
The survivor

By Mia Bailey

Midnight

I wake up
It's 12:00
I crawl out of my bed
And out my window
Into the cold night
Down
Down the tree to the soft ground
To freedom
I hear a noise
Calling me
To run
Through the fields
Jump over fences
Reach to the stars
Sing to the moon
And curl up in the crook
Of a tree
Go to sleep
And dream
And with some help I do
I run through the fields
I jump over fences
I reach to the stars
I sing to the moon
I curl up in the crook
Of a tree
Go to sleep
And dream
I wake up
It's 5:00
I crawl out of my tree
And over to my window
To my warm bed
Up
Up the tree into my window
I go to sleep
As if
It was only a dream
But I know it was real

By Annabelle Flood

Goal

The tie breaker
So close
So far
The ball
So inviting
Comes to me
I wind up
Release
Woooooosh
Smack
The ball is sailing
It's not going to make it
Wait
Wait
It's in the net
In the goal
In the goal
In the goal

By Eric Link

Danse

J'aime danser
Je veux avoir une danse pour les élèves
Avec ma classe
On va voir une danse
Je veux faire une fête à l'école
avec ma classe

By Seynabou Ndiaye

Snapping Turtle

A snapping turtle,
digging a hole in the soil.
Laying eggs,
slippery as oil.
Sitting there on the eggs,
protecting her shelled creatures
She sits there silently.
I stare at her great features
Looking skinny as a bone,
it makes me want to have her chew.
Pulling out grass and roots,
she declines. I leave a few.
Walking away,
I see the moon
Goodbye turtle,
I'll come back soon

By Pierce Tikhon Berry

Alert

A misty morning
In the garden
A deer is staring ahead
Alert
Watching
Standing guard
Protective of her baby
Bushes move
The deer's ears go up
Stiffness
Alert

By Mary Byron

The Basement

In my basement
I found a note
That said move the chair
I did
I found another note
That said take down the rug
I did
There was one last note
That said open the door
I did
I found treasure
I am rich now
Pots and pots of gold
Were in that basement

By Bradley Rosenblatt

Allergies

I got up and smelled the spring air
I went outside
Then I felt a slight tickle in my nose
Aaaaachoo! I sneezed
I went to an oak tree
Aaaaachoo! I sneezed
I went back inside again
Aaaaachoo! I sneezed
Oh how I hate these allergies!

By Benjamin Guo

Lake Champlain

I wake up
I'm sitting at a picnic table
I wonder where I am.
Where could I be?
The wind blows in my face
My hair whips through the air
I hear only the waves crash and
The wind blows through the trees.
I hear the whistle of the wind.
I now know where I am…
I'm at Lake Champlain.

By Marie Sequeira

A Horse

I woke up at night
And looked out my window
I saw a horse
Limp through
My frozen town
It came upon
An abandoned house
So I went outside
And stared at it
I came closer and closer
And started to pet its icy coat
I ran back inside
And got some blankets
But when I came back
The horse was gone.

By Pamela Alcantara

Ferret Fight

The ferrets bounced
He pounced
She jumped and clawed
He got in close
Open to attack
She dodged and clawed
And they left the ferret fight

By Zack Hartke

Elements

Water: I'm a superhero.
All living things need me, including Air.
Without me, it wouldn't really be Air.
Air: Yes, I would!
I'd still be the same without you.
Water: Oh, really?
Air: Really. I would because, without you
I'd still have, uh, um, dangit!
I didn't plan this through.

Water: So, as I was saying…
And Fire, oh devious Fire. No one would
Be able to put him out without me.
Fire: As if you could! You're "Miss
I'm-so-important." Snicker.
Water: Har, har, har. You're so funny
I forgot to laugh.
Fire: Oh, really? Did you forget to, or
Were you jealous that I thought of that first?
Water: Neither. Fire, remember, without me
There would be no Air. And as we both know,
You can't survive without Air. So, Ha!

Earth: What's with all the chatter?
I was trying to sleep.
Water: Sorry, Earth.
Fire: Yeah, sorry. Water was talking a ton.
Water: No, I wasn't.
Fire: Yes, you were.
Earth: I don't care who woke me.

Air: Did you hear? Air is polluted.
Water is trashed. Fires destroy forests.
Earth is heated by greenhouse gases.
Earth: Devastating. Who did this?
Air: People. Some try to help the planet,
but not enough.
So, please, everyone, recycle.
Turn off electricity, and don't litter.

By Alex DeVito

Fifth Grade
Ms. Leonard

Symphony of Sounds

I hear a symphony
A symphony of sounds
A tuba billows and flutes fly around.
I hear the crash of the great bronze gong
The conductor thinks nothing can go wrong.
An array of strings sing through the night
And snare drums beat good night.
A brassy sensation played by trombones
And keyboards play perfect tones.
And oboes lift up and touch the sky,
And now the conductor bows good bye.
The audience spills as trumpets play,
And some guests congratulate.
So now we end the symphony of sounds
So follow your dreams,
And play what you must,
Never
Let your dreams burn down.

By JJ Jennings

Power

Leaders thirsts for
Power
They claim to be leaders
They lie
They crush anything in their path
They kill everyone for power
They will
Kill even you to get it

By Jack Kappler

Running

I love to run.
Running is the best thing in the world.
I love the way you feel,
flying through the air, the world,
and no one is there to tell you to stop,
to wait.
No one dares to talk,
just to watch you fly through life as the girl
That runs.
Run, run, run.
As if no one is there,
Watching
Every step
You take.

By Maddie Bennett

Patience

Patience I
Will find
After
My journey
Through
Kingdoms
My
Patience
Is
Worth
The
Risk.

By Lukas Gose

The Hunger Games

Survival of the fittest,
Running and hiding screaming in pain!
Some choose to fight, and kill instead.
Mourning for your lost friends and wishing
Oh wishing for this to end.
When the people you have known,
All your life watches.....
Back at home everyone knows there's ...
Only going to be one survivor,
and the families prepare to light candles
For the lost
ones
Survival of the fittest

By Caroline Flood

Café to the Rescue

The snowstorm
Pounds me down
I'm frozen solid
Until ...
Two warm hands
Pulls me up to safety
I see a blurry sign-
Café
" Jingle"
The store bell rings
The warmth pours on me
Restoring my body
Another hand grinds
Coffee beans
Into the coffee maker
"Tock"
Goes the clock
While warm coffee
Is being poured into my mouth
Waking me instantly

By Hye Jeong Yun

Morning

I was sleeping peacefully
Until Ring! Ring! Ring!
My alarm went off and I woke up
I yawned,
Still tired but refreshed
From a good night's sleep
As I stretched,
The sun rose
And it
Glittered and glowed like gold
In the early morning

By Ryan Smith

The Thunder Hawk

The mighty Thunder Hawk
Soars over the hills
With powerful wings
Cows and ponies grazing below
Cower in fear of
The mighty Thunder Hawk

By Rebecca Nelson

The Fire King

The Fire King burned
as clear as crystal
on coal

By Mitch Laughlin

The Fall

The canyon
So far below me
How deep?
50 feet?
100?
But the view
It's amazing
I can't help but cling to the edge
The canyon isn't as deep here
I look down
The earth under my foot crumbles
No
How?
I watched the trail
I never set foot on an overhang
But here I am
The blood drumming in my ears
As I fall
I hit the earth
I whirl thunders through my head
But I must get out
My hands and knees are scraped
But I must get out
Do I call for help?
But who would respond?
I MUST get out
First one foot
Then the other
My ankle Buckles
The Pain races through my legs
Like tiny electrodes
Running through my veins
I MUST GET OUT
I try again
I face the pain and clench my teeth
My hands are scraped
They sting as I scale the canyon wall
I can do this
I have to
I MUST

GET
OUT!
Fiery pain fills every step
I keep going
I reach the top
My friends are there
They searched for me
When I didn't come back
"What happened?"
They ask
I say nothing
I look back into the canyon where I fell
But that doesn't change anything
Because I survived
The Fall

By Maria Pieruccini

No Need for Money

Wealth, decays time
Wealth is what you don't need where the dead go
Time is what you need to survive

By Christian Ro

The Wreck

I often think of that
moment
when I was in the backseat
the rain
pounding away like a sledgehammer
the windshield wipers trying
their best to vanquish the rain
and then…
There was the wreck.

By Winston Evans

Bully

Joey
Hates being
Bullied
He goes around the
Corner
To his great
Alley
With his friends
But then the
Bullies
Come to pick
On Joey and
His friends.
But
Joey stands up for
Himself.
He tells them to
"STOP"
Picking on him and his friends.
The bullies
Want to fight them
But then the
Principal
Comes and
"STOPPED"
The fight.

By Damon Johnson

The Pebble

The fast slick river
carves the rock
making it look like a house
sitting on a pebble
lifting the world on its shoulders.

By Jake Hoetmer

Snow

I am very excited
As I watch the
Silver snow
Fall to the
Icy ground.
It doesn't kill anything.
It just preserves happiness,
In a frozen
Block of ice.

By Brendan Furness

The Flower Dancer

Like a petal
Gently floating down with the wind
She dances
Restlessly
The routine
Is not plain
But is
An explosion
Of magnificent colors

By Jillian Fan

The Golden Mist
Pollen
Circles around me
It is a
Golden mist
I am
Alone
With my
Allergies
Stuck
Until the
Pollen gets
Washed away
With the next rain.
By Patrick Lovelace

There once was…
There once was…
A pig named Joe
A guy who said so
A dog that was blue
A unicorn that ate glue
A chicken that could lie
A cat that could fly
A dog named Yoda
A can of soda
A jar full of tar
A game called par

A house with a loft
A shirt that is soft
A big calculator
A word called later
A time to read a book
A chicken fried by a cook
And as you can see
A guy named MEEEEE!!!
By Akrit Sinha

Time
Time's sand falls through his fingers
he excites as he plays
the earth game with us
one of us wastes away from time
he laughs at the death
with the power of thunder
By Devon Hunt

Food
The glistening moon
Showers on me
As I sneak into the
House on the
Table brighter than
The moon
Tortillas
By Liam Corrado

My Dream
In my dream
A light breeze passes
Through the air making the cherry blossom
Tree shake
As the petals fall to the ground
I open my eyes
And instantly my dream goes
Away
By Aishwarya Jadhav

Life

Part One

The splashes of white,
Cascades of red,
Sprinkles of pink,
And flashes of beauty
All swirled into
One Dogwood flower
A soft breeze ruffles
Each petal
And the Dogwood flower
Sways
A dance so short
Yet so beautiful
Every sunrise, sunset, moonrise, and midnight
Lights or shadows
The Dogwood flower
With beauty
Unparalleled
And unique
The splashes of white
Cascades of red and sprinkles of pink
Form the one and only
Dogwood flower

Part Two

With each passing day
And each passing night
The Dogwood flower
Flourishes
Always more beautiful
Than its previous self
As is soaks in the morning sun
The Dogwood flower relaxes
Taking in each moment
Clinging to it
Like you would
A fading dream
In the morning
Each moment is precious
Because the Dogwood flower knows

Sherry Xie

That each dawn
Could be its last
Maybe this is why
A Dogwood flower is
Content with life
Whereas humans
Are not

Part Three

The Dogwood flower's soft breeze
Becomes a gale
As spring and sun
Give way
To devastating
Storms
Each Dogwood flower
Grasps their branch
For dear life
Watching

As their family
Get torn
Off their branches
Into the howling wind
That has no heart
Finally
Even the strongest flowers
Can't hold back death
And as they join their families
They scroll through their
Happiest memories
One last time
At last the storm is silenced
No one bothers
To mourn the Dogwood flowers
Scattered, frozen, muddy, corpses
Part Four
No survivors are left
Yet the next generation
Still embrace life
For the happiness
And joy
It brings
Life
Is like the Dogwood flower
Sweet
Yet not long-lasting
But so
Pleasant
With the time you have
Make a difference
Do good
Help the world
Leave a fingerprint
That lasts
Do like the Dogwood flower
Realize what it means to live
Cherish each moment
And never forget
The meaning of life
By Sherry Xie

Diamonds
At dawn,
When the first rays of sunlight hit those little
Cracks in the ground,
When the glittering moon dies down into the
Ground like mother earth is swallowing it,
When the diamonds glitter,
When the children come out to play they
Hide themselves as if to hide from the
Sunlight reflecting off the children's
Sunglasses
By Meghan Parmer

Summer
I lie down
Sleepy.
Under the shade
Of the trees.
Avoiding the heat,
And mosquitoes,
That could burn me.
By Amanda Mitchell

Ode to my Mother:
On a gloomy day,
I stare out the
Window.
Feeling sad.
But then,
I see your
Reflection.
Beaming at me.
I turn around
And smile at you.
Because you know
Exactly
How to cheer me up.
So let's go back in time,
To the time
When you bought me
My first doll,
And I jumped up and down,
Dancing around the room.
To the time
When I went on
The big, scary
Roller Coaster.
And you held me tight,
The whole ride.
You were always there for me.
Through the hardest times.
As a mother, you are
Loving,
Caring,
Thoughtful,
And kind.
You are the one
Who goes with me
To shop,
To talk,
And to laugh together.
My favorite moments
Are always with you.
Because you are

A Mother.
The B-E-S-T mother
In the world.
By Candace Miu

The King
As the king sat down on his
red velvet chair
he watched the fire crackle and
pop
the coal
a burning sensation
holding his golden crown
wondering
wondering when his son would
take over the throne
By Lexi Novak

Sorrowful Pasture
A hawk glides
Over a soaked landscape
As a wild mustang
Streaks over an elevated pasture
Thunder rumbles in the distance
Like an echo dying slowly
By Kristin Giery

The Time Stained Memory

Ivy streaks through a maze of cracked bricks
Shattered glass layers the untamed plants
That recoil against the shards of glass which
Repeat a memory of lost hopes
The roof lay ruptured no longer shielding
Its gaping hole peering in on the empty
House
Full of despair
That the soil still grasps in its weak,
Tear-stained hands
The neighbors have forgotten
But the victim can't forget
The landowners plunged into an epidemic
A dreamless sleep
That ticks, ticks, ticks
into the forgotten
World of unfaithful souls
They died twenty years ago from the fever
Leaving us hoping we could die with them
Death was only thing that could save us now
And peel us from the tight grasp of the
Forgotten who stabbed us and speared us with
the sharpest blades of sadness in
which we cry tears breaking us
a p a r t
one
by
one
We an abyss
Thinly layered by showers
of despair and
Emptiness as we fall
Deeper
Deeper
Reaching the impact at
the bottem
The land of the
Forgotten

By Sophia Dietz

Fifth Grade
Mr. Montaquila

T-Rex
T-Rex
Freakishly huge
T-Rex
Not smart
I love T-Rexes,
T-Rex kills its prey
T-Rex eats
The T-Rex is now thirsty
It get's its drink of water
It's set to go
But wait!
What's that in the sky?
Then boom!
T-Rex falls over.
T-Rex's bones will be found for the whole wide
world to see!
By Matthew Dukes

My Brother
I love my brother a lot
It breaks my heart when we fight
I love it when we get along
He makes me smile and I make him smile
We make fun of each other
(not in the mean way)
We have fun and fights
But that is just the way we are
I love you Tristan!
You are my whole world!
By Ariel Cooper

Little Owl
Little Owl,
Everywhere
Hooting hooting
Everywhere!!
Little Owl
Fly at night,
Shiny star's in the sky
Twinkle in the Owl's little eyes.
Little Owl fly's through the night!!!
By Christina Cortes

Sushi
Sushi is so good
Awesome with soy sauce
Fish, seaweed and rice
Together so good
People say it is raw fish
I say
I like raw fish!
By Yousef Elmuhtaseb

Summer
Summer! Summer!
Too HOT to play outside
Mom comes barging in my room
Yelling get up and READ!
NO!!
I want to go to the pool!
By Sohale Hessavi

The Beach

The sandy sandy shore
With lots of seagulls
All in the sky,
I smell the salty water
And see the waves hit the shore
I sit in my beach chair and under my
Umbrella
Eating goldfish,
Watching a shark swim
Into the deep,
I see a child building a sand castle
And watch it disappear into
The water

By Brooke Balducci

Lacrosse

Dad yelling
Me rushing
Zooming to the field
Pass the ball
Play monkey in the middle
We have a scrimmage
Score a goal
Drive home
Mom asks
How was your day?

By Noah Smith

Fruits

Fruits
Oh fruits
You are so good for me
Banana you have a peel
Not my favorite but ok
You too orange and grape
Your taste is so good
And you coconut
You're hard and I don't like the taste of you
Apple your good enough for me
And watermelon you are my favorite
And pear you stink
Strawberry you are so yummy
But not as good as watermelon
Fruits
You are EPIC

By Norris Gallagher

The Beach

The beach is filled with fun,
With dolphins
And buckets of sand
And shovels for making sand castles
A day at the beach is a
Fun,
Fun,
Fun Day

By Meredith Vitanza

Key West

Key West
I love it's beaches,
the clear blue water,
the soft yellow sand,
people snorkeling watching the fish,
people kayaking paddling strong,
and people surfing catching waves,
there is always someone in the Key West blues!

By Isabel Viner

The Three Cateers

I have 3 cats
The Cateers
First is Cookie
Also known as Cookie monster
He is white like the snow
He jumps off walls and sneaks like a ninja
His meow makes him sound like he's Spanish
Cookie loves to snuggle like a teddy bear
He may crawl under the covers of my bed
In the middle of the night and scratch my legs
But still,
You have to love the cookie monster
My second is Bootser
Nickname: Bootscat
We all think of her as a soccer ball
She looks as if she swallowed one!
She's black and white,
White on her paws and stomach
In the middle of the night she runs around
Carrying her toy mouse
Howling, howling, waking us all up.
She may also give me a bad night's sleep
But you have to love the soccer ball.
Last, but not least
Is Oreo
We usually call her Mew, Mew
When she's hungry for her Friskies she goes
Mew! Mew!
She is practically a mini Bootser
Every morning I wake up to see little Oreo on
My face
When I hold her she looks up at me with her
Big eyes
Her little timid paws
When she lies down her legs
Stick out from under her
When she climbs up the back of the sofa
POOF!
She appears
All together they are
Cookie monster
Bootscat
Mew, Mew
The 3 Cateers

By Sarah Heymsfeld

Swimming

The cold rush as I dive
into the
water for my
25 fly
I'm racing to the finish
I lift my head to breathe
I hear cheering
SPLASH!!!
I touch the wall
and
my time stops!!!
I WON MY RACE!!

By Madeline LaPorte

Dragon

Dragon, Dragon
In the Sky
Dragon, Dragon
Flying High
Dragon, Dragon
Big Red Eye
CIVILIZATION YOU WILL DIE!!!

By Christopher van der Veer

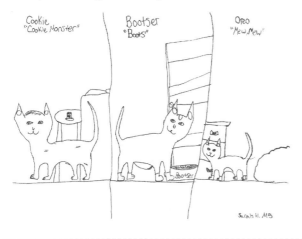

My Cousin's House

Sometimes
I visit my cousin's house
Way down in Florida
The hot creamy weather
Makes my mouth water and
My face sweat
As I open the door
The dogs run toward me
Welcoming me in
Giving me comfort
Inside the warm house
I watch T.V
In the warm cozy blankets
By the chair
The boxer dogs lick me
Happily and wildly
Climbing on my knees
When I smell the sweet sent
Of…
Dinner
I know it's ready
My aunt yells
"IT'S READY!"

By Elizabeth Laxton

Crazy Yellow Dog

Yep,
That's Trixie,
My crazy yellow dog,
She runs around like crazy,
Until you play fetch with her,
Or sometimes even,
On a walk,
When you're on a walk,
Just be ready to see something crazy,
She will find a,
BRANCH!
She will take it until you make her,
DROP!
When she sees a squirrel,
She will stare at it!
Sometimes,
she will try to get it!
When the walk is over,
She lies on the cold tile floor,
You can hear her breathing,
VERY, VERY,
Heavily,
I tell her to get water,
She goes and drinks until,
The bowl,
Is empty,
That's Trixie,
My crazy yellow dog!

By Samantha Lowe

Space Penguin

There once was a penguin
Who was shot into space
And then
Saw something that made it quack
In fear
It was an alien in a…
U.F.O

By Oliver Smitt-Jeppesen

Bingo
Beast
Intelligent
Nuts
Giant
O-mazing

Bingo is a velcro
Bingo is a spaz
That's my 90 pound bubba
Woof! Woof!

By Jenna Shuey

The Monkey
Monkey monkey had a big frown
Monkey monkey rampage the town
Monkey monkey found a banana
Monkey monkey it was too small
Monkey monkey said
THE WORLD WILL FALL!!!

By Sammy Rzonca

My Kobe Jersey
Man, when I got my Kobe jersey
I yelled and shouted
I thought I would faint
But my mom would have pouted.
I was so happy and my hands got clappy!
I looked at it with great care
If dust got on it
I would have died.
The Adidas sign looked so cool
I started to drool.
I put it on and ran till dawn.
I felt so good
I knew I could,
Play basketball differently.
I LOVE that jersey!

By Evan Pascal

My Dog Jada
Jada
Who is a dog
Who is under a year old
Who loves people, dogs, and cats
Who feels happy, playful, and hungry
Who needs walks, a playmate, and a chew toy
That she can't break
Who gives love
Who fears vacuums, TVs and my little sister
Who would like to see the world's biggest bone!
Who shares toys (not always)
Who is skinny
Who lives in this neighborhood
Pew

By Griffin Pew

Slurpee
Slurpee
Oh Slurpee
You are the best thing to slurp
Something to slurp after school
7-11 is the place I will find you
Until next time SLURPEE

By Jakub Rogers

Slurpees
Slurpees Slurpees everywhere!
Tasty, tasty, tasty!
Every color of the rainbow!
So good!
Change your mood!
Down in the dumps?
Drink a Slurpee!
Got a bad haircut?
Drink a Slurpee!
Taste the love!

By Owen Steele

Cup Cakes

Cup cakes
My favorite
Yum! Yum!
It's delicious
It is a good strawberry cup cake

By Shaheem Peterson

Space Llama

Space Llama
Found Space Penguin on mars
Space Llama
Wound his way through the cave and
Started wars on mars
In the end Space Llama won

By Justin Plummer

The Night Sky

The black sky covers the land
with the bright stars
and the beaming shooting star
the glowing moonlight
they all cover
the night sky

By Sarah Wolfe

The Flower

I found a flower
that fell from the gentle sky
that's just laying down
on that green lily pad

By Ally McMonagle

Runescape

High peaks, low peaks
High levels, low levels
Good people, bad people
Good armor, bad armor
More money
Less money
Good guardians
Bad guardians
Favored by people
Not favored by people
Good computers
Bad computers
Amazing Runescape

By Benjamin Hull

Animals

Animals in the desert
Animals in the ocean
Animals in the jungle
Look at that motion
There are animals on rocks
and in trees
and under water
and on leaves!
I love animals
I like them a lot
Poor thing, in a pot
I'm sorry poor thing
You are cute
But. . . . "Hoot! Hoot!"
WOW!!!! That is an awesome sound!
I LOVE ANIMALS!!!!

By Kristina Macaluso

Runescape

Runes you can use to do magic
Underground dungeons
Numerous beasts
Enter wars
Saradomin
is who the people pray for help
Clans that you can join
Always a lot of fun
People wear different kinds of armor
Everyone can duel in a dueling arena

By Soren Jouanneau

Ms. Burkman

Multi-Grade Class 4–6

A pple
L augh
E xcited
e Xcellent

lavcgh 800

L augh
O nion
R at
E at
N ote
Z oo
O range

L uwfe
U merebella
M onastary
A ustralia
W ashengton DC

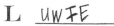

J ump
O range
R un
D rum
A pple
N ap

T A
O R A N G E
M A N G O
M S C D L E O
Y O H U S O L
   N G E T

Sixth Grade
Ms. Diebold

Baseball
I enjoy Baseball
Sometimes you will fall
Rarely

Come to a great game
They're never the same
Vary

My pants get dirty
I'm number thirty
Very

By Sebastian Ainspan

Clumsy
William Brock
Was as fast as a rock
I've seen snails outrun him
I think he needs some time at the gym

Mr. Brock
Jumped off the dock
He tried to do a belly flop
But he landed on his pop

Brock, Will
Tripped and fell down a hill
He rolled into a lake
And was bit by a water snake

By Drew Crum

Weird People
Christopher Port
Is a good sport
Although he is glad
His grades are awfully bad

Derrick Jeek
Has a large beak
He likes to text
And eat insects

Richie Sunny
Had lots of money
He bought fifty million socks
Now he lives in a box

B.B. Boffee
Loved to drink coffee
She was so hyper
She moved quickly as a viper

By Jordan Gamarra

My Guinea Pig Ate My Homework
I was doing my homework
My guinea pig came and ate it

Why he did it I don't know
But he ate it

Sorry I didn't do #25
My guinea pig ate my home work

By David Joyner

Wings

Flying in the sky
Birds are passing by
A dream

Soaring through the air
Glide without a care
So high

Feel the wind rushing
Around as you dive
For a fluffy cloud

The sun sets with a
Burst of radiant colors
Night blankets the world

Wings can take you far
Up into the stars
It's a great chance
To dance and to prance
While looking down at cars

Moon shining above
City lights glinting below
In the evening sky

Ring a little bell
Things can be done well
With wings

By Sindhu Ranga

Dogwood Tree

The dogwood tree sways softly in the breeze,
Its petals float across the meadow,
In a daydream.
The clouds fly,
Away from here,
To make way for clear spring days.
As the dogwood tree petals float,
As the clouds fly,
The baby robin hatches,
And spring begins.

By Megan Reilly

The Oceanside

Many grains of sand
The end of the land
Huge, clear
Strong waves that are deep
Hit rocks that are steep
No fear
Watch the dolphins play
They will play all day
All year

By Peter Almanza

Black Swans

In a world devoid of darkness
There lies no shame
Everything floats light and airy
No one is to blame

Jealousy remains a rock unturned
And all stare fearlessly on
And no anger burns in various pits
Only superficial joy moves pawns

Hark, the angel sings her song
Yet her words breathe no life
Because here lives no hunger nor strife

And in this land thou cast not a shadow
And good has no company
No black to her white
No war to her peace

May one day come black swans upon this nation
So a few shadows of doubt may creep
Rocks may be turned
Pits may glow in fiery light
So that
The angels may breathe life
And good may have company

Only when the black swans come

By Klara Vertes

Natural Skyscrapers

Walking through this forest
My feet padding softly on the ground
I feel like a tiny speck.
The redwood trees
Tower high above me.
The leaves whisper in the breeze,
The birds twitter high above.
As I try to glimpse the top of these giants,
My head slowly tilts backwards
And my eyes finally reach
The highest branch.
I stare upwards,
Not believing the height
Of this natural skyscraper.

By Lucy Nguyen

Paradise

My idea of paradise is,
No school or jobs
Everybody lives in mansions
Endless supply of cash
Everybody's normal
Snowing all day every day
Money grows on trees
Nobody dies
Not hot, not cold
World peace
No hungry people
So, how do I make it happen?

B: Chad Constantine

Cool Weird Dudes

The Jamaican mon,
Ate a honey bon.
Jake luke
Was a Jamaican,
He fried bacon
Bob Duke
Was from Canada,
He owned fat Pandas.
Cool dudes
From around the world,
Are really weird,
And cool.

By Jishnu Medisetti

Mr. Doughnut

He looks so yummy
Get in my tummy
I dream

He looks like sweet pea
Eyes glaring at me
The cream

Saying please don't eat
I'm not a good treat
Not lean

By Andrew McClellan

A Beach

The waves,
Deep and green
Wash over me
Serene.

Across the sandy shore
Shells are strewn
But it is so much more
A graveyard for the fallen sea.

Scuttling sideways,
Clumsy and bizarre
I watch the hermits
From afar.

Wind tugs at the kite
It wants to be free
Flying away
From the beach and me.

Seagulls cry
An eerie sound
Loud and sharp
Heard for miles around.

The beach, though dead
Still harbors life
For life goes on
So have no strife.

By Sierra Davis

The Dog and the Fiddle

Hey little diddle the dog and the fiddle
A duck nearly jumped the sun
He got burnt to crisp
Because he missed
And you won't be seeing him soon

By Frank Kwartin

I can be

I can be a lawyer
I can be a doctor
I can be a fireman
I can be a musician
I can be an engineer
I can be a teacher
I can be an actor
I can be what I want to be
But that's my choice

By Nathan Nkomba

Humpty Dumpty

Humpty Dumpty sat on a wall
Humpty Dumpty had a great fall
He fell on his back
And got a big crack
And that was the end of Humpty's attack

By Brooke O'Donnell

Ashes
Once they were a huge fire
Lighting the night sky
With people around it
Cuddling warm
The joy
The laughter

The people make smores
So delicious to eat
Sweet

The fire dies
Late into the night
Now only
Ashes
Remain
By: Ana Stanisavljev

Sometimes I Wish
Sometimes I wish I had wings
Sometimes I wish I could fly
Sometimes I wish I could jump
Like a frog
Pick my feet off the ground and
Touch the stars
Swing around
As I watch the small towns and little people
By Annika Gude

How I Live
I wake up today
And live life my way
A choice

Feeling very good
And saying I could
I live

I'm happy and sad
I'm good and I'm bad
My life
By Delaney Connolly

The Night Sky
The stars are gleaming
With special meaning
It looks
The moon is giant
So far and distant
It seems
Every single night
I turn my head right
The sky
By: Charles Velarde

Trees
Trees are green
Trees are lean
O! Those beautiful trees
Are covered in fleas

By Zeid Diab

Cherry Trees
Spring is the awakening
The pink blossoms come to shine
Shed off their beauty to the world
Forever will they be
A peace of art

The sun gleams down
Pink flowers glow softly
A gentle breeze rustles the leaves
The sweet smell of cherry blossoms fills the air
The birds sing their melodies
The breeze carries the flowers
into the river
As the world looks in
awe…
At the Cherry Trees
By Kristin Putman

Bennie's Gum

Bennie S. Wumm
Sticks sticky gum
To the bottom of desks
During extremely long tests

By Evan Parker

The Game

"PASS!" I scream
My teammate inbounds the ball to me
I run down the court
10 seconds on the clock
My team's down by 2 points
I look up the court
Nobody's open
My time to shine
8 seconds
I get past half-court
I do a crossover, behind the back dribble
The defender is too good
3 seconds
I fake drive and pull up for the 3 pointer
The buzzer goes off
Everyone is silent as the orange ball spins perfectly through the air
Then "Swish"
The crowd groans since my team is away
My teammates tackle me
We've won the game

By Rohan Wente

Adrenalin

I run down the court,
My adrenalin is pumping,
I feel a trickle of sweat,
My heart is thumping,

Everything depends,
Upon this shot,
Maybe I'll miss,
Maybe not,

To be the best,
We needed this winning,
My mouth is dry,
My head is spinning,

I take my chances,
And throw towards the basket,
I'm sure,
I'll soon be in a casket,

The ball goes in,
I hear a roar,
And screams and cheers,
I really scored!

By: Victoria Slaski

Ducks, Dogs, and Frogs. Oh My!

Did you hear
The duck that quacked
A ferocious quack
A quack so loud and terrible
Grown men would run and hide
At the very sound

Did you see
The dog that was so hideous
He resembled a beast
With sharp long fangs
and beady black eyes
the bravest lions
cowered in his presence
did you smell
the frog that had the most dreadful odor
he smelled of slime and mold
an odor so terrible and pungent
skunks ran from him
ducks dogs and frogs
OH MY!

By Page Murray

The Doughnut

The succulent doughnut,
Don't think of a what,
I dream

Glazed, Chocolate, so good,
They are not booed,
It seems

Have flavors I love,
It is like a dove,
I mean

By Nikhil Rao

Sixth Grade
Mrs. Kunkle

The Tiger
The Tiger saw the light.
The light was very bright.
The brightness created blindness,
The blindness made him see no brightness.
His future is no longer bright.

By Jessica Lister

Sun
It was mellow and yellow.
It was big, and wasn't a stick.
It first shone south, then west.
Then all over,
It tries to look big!

By Alex Danielsson

The Cat in the Hat with a Dog
There once was a cat playing with a hat.
Then came a dog; a big fat one.
The dog grabbed the hat,
The cat jumped in,
So did the dog!

By Safy El-Nahal

Penguins
Baby penguins are so cute.
They're as sweet as fruit!
Older penguins are fast in water,
I hope they don't get slaughtered!
Also, they don't wear boots!

By Hope Mayo

Chocolate
I love chocolate.
It is a piece of heaven.
It makes me happy!

By Abby Wickman

Hello
As she walks around,
she says "hi"
to everyone in her path.
She says "bye"
to the ones that she's passed.

She's looking around
at the world that
surrounds her.
The vibrant colors;
all so beautiful.

Such a sight to see.
The mountains beyond the horizon
and the sun setting
as she walks home.
All this at her finger tips.

By Kailey Zamborsky

Squirt
My Pal is named Squirt,
We enjoy shnacks and shlurpys.
Me and Squirt are pals!

By Emma Youngren

Name the Dinosaur
Daspletosaurs
Indosaurus
Nemegtosaurus
Ornithomimus
Stenopelix
Acrocanthosaurus
Utahraptor
Riojasaurus

By Seretha McHugh

Seretha McHugh K/6

Candy
Candy is…
sweet and sour.
You get that,
tasty sensation
in your mouth.
Lollipops,
Jolly Ranchers,
Hard Candy,
Chewables.
But favorite of all…
Twizzlers!

By Matt Hughes

Dream
There was a dog named dream.
Dream married Ice Cream!
With a spoon and a knife,
He took her life!
Oh! That poor Ice Cream!

By Maddie Hill

The Guy Who Went Splat
A guy was sitting,
on a rainbow over clouds.
The guy fell and…SPLAT!

By Clayton Bowling

Rufus
Hello, I'm a cat!
My name is Rufus, oh.
I like me fishie!

By Calista Gasper

I Like Potatoes
Potato, Potato…
You're big, red tomato is so
big and juicy!
And…
big and fat and hairy!
I like tomato,
Potato,
Rotato Flato!

By Ty Brazell

Fruit Full of Fun
Tango with a Mango,
Tap dance with a Banana,
Get dairy with a Cherry,
Get bored with an Orange
Share with a Pear,
Have a fruit!
Have fun and just don't care!

By Christina Adlam

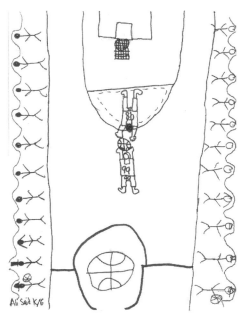

NBA

SCORE!!!
The bouncing of the ball,
the shooting,
the strength.
Great power makes
great responsibility.
Do the John Wall;
practice,
work hard to win games!

SCORE!!!
Again!
Sometimes you get
crazy over it.
But it's a lot of fun.
Unlike how some people like
the NFL.
The throwing of the smoke,
with Lebron and the pull-ups
on the basket with Wade.

SCORE!!!
I'm all out of agains.
What a huge game,
with the rosters like the
big 4 in Boston.
Who's the fifth?
How about the Championships?
Everyone has been going through
like the Lakers
back-to-back championships.
The game finally ended…
in triple overtime.
It was a game for everyone!

By Ali Said

Spotty

There was a Turtle that had a shell,
and Spotty was his name, oh!
S-P-O-T-T-Y
And Spotty was his name, oh!

There was a turtle that had a tank,
and Spotty was his name, oh!
S-P-O-T-T-Y
And Spotty was his name, oh!

There was a turtle that swam around,
and Spotty was his name, oh!
S-P-O-T-T-Y
And Spotty was his name, oh!

By Blake Bond

Ice Cream Pie

Ice cream pie tastes good!
Apple pie is not as good.
I love ice cream pie!

By JJ Carlson

Bee-Very Fast!

Along came a bee,
So I ran and so did he!
We ran and ran, as fast as we could.
Would I scream? Of course I would!
And the bee? It just ran into a tree!
(I hate bees!)

By Kelly Le

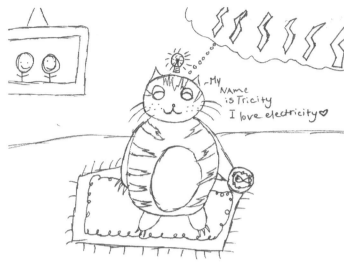

Ode to a Lunch Box

Every day I just sit,
sit doing nothing.
Going back and forth
from school and home.
My travel being a rotten,
stink, squished old backpack.

Sometimes I think and say in my head,
"Why? Why me?
What is the point of my life!"
People putting stuff in me all the time.

Sometimes I say to myself,
"What is the point in this?
Having rotten, stinky food inside of me."
What is the point in life of a…
Lunch Box!

By Erin Gray

The Fat Cat

There was a cat named Tricity,
He loved electricity.
He loved to eat fish,
On his pretty dish.
He died of obesity.

By Elif Thompson

Bananas

Me like banana.
Me like banana more!
Monkey, Banana!

By Tarun Singh

Cat

I look out the window;
all I can see
three little
tempting mice
looking at me.

The kitty I am,
I love to play.
I hunt and I pounce,
all night
and all day.

I get up
from the window.
Sprint from the house!
I pounce,
I capture,
I gobble the mouse.

By Ellie Crump

Drops of Rain

Every drop of rain is like a thought,
because we have so many.

When it rains softly,
it means there are not as many thoughts.
But when it rains hard,
the thoughts come pouring down.

Every little droplet is completely different.
Every little thought has a mind of its own.

By Rebecca Fisher-Tringale

Doll
As she danced for masked humans,
her aquamarine eyes were shining
and rimmed with bright wet tears of fear…

She tripped over her feet and fell over,
her string had broken.
The masked humans laughed at her.

More of her crystal tears poured out.
They were hot down her porcelain cheeks…

Yet it was her imagination.
Her strings were too tight to break
and tears couldn't pour out,
as she was a doll.
A lifeless being,
emotions are void…

She is a puppet for the living.

By Tiffany Tran

Sixth Grade

Mr. Parker

A New Beginning
The first fire broke the silence
And the war began.
The smoke
Darkened the clouds
Above us.
Minutes later,
The village became crippled
And plastered
With cannon balls and bullets.
Us villagers were devastated,
Scared,
Sad,
Furious,
Until we saw
A bright, white light
Hovering above us.
A glowing angel
With feathered wings
In the center
Of the bright light.
It was a good sign
Of recovery
And a great future.

By Shiling Zhao

Popcorn
CRUNCH! CRUNCH!
My mouth explodes
With tasty butter,
The movie doesn't
Matter
It is
You,
My love and inspiration
Your light and fluffy
Shell covered with
Yellow butter
Is all I can think
About
I think I am in
Love,
With popcorn
You melt my
My heart into lovely
Butter
And you fill my
Head with grainy
Puff balls,
Oh no, you are gone,
My hands feel the bottom
Of your red striped bag
But wait,
Free refills!

By Nikita Sawant

My Decision
I hope it was worth it
I had sacrificed everything I had
For the golden rope
"It was magical," the trader boasted
Now, I was one tiny handshake away

From my path to destiny
An idea formed in my mind
"Look!" I yelled. "A monster!"
He turned and I let my dog out to distract him
Then, I ran away and my dog followed me

By Akshat Chopra

Cycles of the Sky
A three part poem
Inspired by Sandy Lyne

I.

The sun,
rising
in the east,
floods the sky,
with colors
of sunrise

The wind,
slowly dies down,
putting
the water
to rest
as it gets warmer
throughout the day

As the sun,
slowly
makes its way
westward,
across the sky,
and
the blooms
open up
to harness
the sun's
heat
and light

When the sun
finally sets,
and the wind
starts to blow,
it taunts
the water
to lap up
against the rock
to carve
the rock ,
and when the wind
is gone,
ready
to come
another day,
then sunrise,
is once more

II.

The sun,
completing its journey
in the east,
it slowly sets
in the west

The blooms
are slowly
closing,
put to rest
and they slowly
disappear
and are nothing
but buds

The sky,
turns
a bluish hue
and I
find fault
in the winter moon,
for turning
the sky
so beautiful

The winter moon
is in
its most beautiful
phase,
full moon

It is shining,
as blue
as Lapis-
lazuli,
a deep blue,
with its golden
shimmer
preceding any stars
around it
forever shining,
in its amazing luster

A little crystal,
in the sky,
and the precious
moonlight
more valuable
than diamond
shines
through my window

III.

The sun
chariot,
begins
its journey
leisurely,
from east,
to west

It feeds
the blooms
with sky food
and the warmth,
after,
a cold night,
of rising wind
shaking
its petals
almost off
of the flower
nearly
ripping
them apart

As,
I sit
on my balcony
to slowly
take it all
in,
the roses
catching
my eye,
so red,
so yellow,
so pink,
and orange

And those anxious,
little,
robins
hopping
from branch,
to branch
and they sing
their song

By Yashaswini Makkena

Autumn Leaves
It's autumn
The leaves on the trees
Are the colors
Of dragon fire
They are beautiful
But soon the fire will
Turn to smoke
And float away
By Rachel Martinka

The Tree and the Cat
The tree is waiting for the cat
When the cat shows up it turns fat
The cat finds a kite
and they start to fight
right until the cat see's a rat
By Nicholas Ramirez

Through the Ears
A black and white land
In front of myself,
The only two colors that I see
Are the two plainest around,
But when my fingers fall upon
The piano keys
In front of me
A MILLION COLORS
Spring to life,
Though not through the eyes…
But, through the ears
By Marie Fontenot

The Amazing Eraser
I love eresers
OOPS!
I love er sers
I love erasers
There we go!
And that is the power
Of the amazing eraser
By Ali Jelvani

No Words
I run
Barefoot
In the green,
Towards the
Sunrise
No words can
Describe this feeling
By Lexi Warner

Annoying Cats

My cats are annoying sometimes
They try to eat all of my dimes
They meow me awake
Should be dunked in a lake
Or maybe just squirted with limes

By Chris Cortese

Coke

Coke goes down
Your throat
It is sugary
It is sweet
A liquid from the
Heavens
Made in factories
But still so sweet
It drips down my throat
Way to fast
Sip by sip
Fraction by fraction
Soon it is gone.
But
It was oh so good to drink.

By Quang Nguyen

A Fairy

A lily pad a fairy sits upon
As she waits for morning's
Sparkling dawn
Dressed in azalea's crisp pink petals
She jingled her jewelry
Of precious metals
Her wings as soft as dandelion seeds
Her bare feet tickled by blowing weeds
Her voice as gentle as trickling water
She is the sun and the moon's
Most faithful daughter
At night her glow is sparkling and bright
As she wards off shadows
With her twinkling light
She listens to the forests
Dark hidden stories
But also listens to its admirable glories
She flies among the purple moors
Purple heather
Her sunlit wild eyes
The color of a peacock's feather
As the sun starts to set
She paints the sky
Her soft corals, peaches, and purples
No one can decry
She sleeps through nights dark
And wakes before morn
To watch early birds
Pick at worms
In the lawn
A lily pad a fairy sits upon
As they wait for morning's
Sparkling dawn
Dressed in azalea's crisp pink petals…

By Autumn Anthony

Mental Walls

Even though
The bombs
Are coming,
Nobody panics.
Everyone hides,
Behind their mental shield,
Thinking they
Are protected.
But nobody notices
The holes.
When their shield falters,
They try their escapes,
But their wall,
The wall that they created
Is holding them back.

By Heather Whittaker

Flying
My heart fills with sorrow
as I watch the perching birds
leave their branches and soar.
I wish that, like the birds, I could fly,
but I know it is impossible.
Heartbroken, I fill with remorse.

Disheartened, my remorse
and sorrow
grow, for I know it is impossible
for me to fly like the birds.
I will never fly
nor soar.

To soar,
just for a second, would take away my remorse,
for if I can soar, I can fly,
and with the wind, it would blow away
my sorrow.
I would dip and do air tricks with the birds,
And the feat of flying would no longer be
impossible.

Why are things impossible?
Why can't we, as humans, soar with the birds,
for our problems would be solved, and gone
would be the remorse
mixed in with the sorrow
that we have because we cannot fly.

I wonder what it feels like to fly.
To imagine it today is impossible,
and this triggers our sorrow.
Oh, how I would love to soar,
far above the horrible remorse,
with the birds.

The birds
make it look so easy to fly,
unlike the remorse
that comes with the fact that flying without the
help of a vehicle is impossible.
I would be ecstatic if I could soar,
but I cannot, and back comes my sorrow.

The sorrow coming with the fact that birds can
soar and fly and that is impossible for us to does
not affect me anymore.
No more remorse flows through me, for I know
that one day I will fly
as well.

By Jack Lovelace

Ode to Baseball
Baseball
The best sport
In the universe
Played with a white ball
With red seams on it
Played between two teams
For nine innings
Played with a glove
And a baseball bat
With a pitcher
That throws the ball
With a batter
Who tries to hit the ball
With a fielder
Who tries to catch the ball
On a giant field
With a diamond of dirt
With four bases
1st, 2nd, 3rd and home
With the fans
In the stands
Cheering for their favorite team
And eating hot dogs and crackerjack
Baseball
America's Pastime
Is the best sport in the universe

By Bryan Kim

Alice

Following the rabbit's trail
She knows not of what will happen
But down the rabbit hole she goes
Not knowing what else to do
She starts to explore

She meets the Dodo Bird
The Mock Turtle
And the Door Mouse
Together they have
A Caucus race
A silly sort of sport

There she meets
The Red Queen
Vain in every way
Then she meets
The White Queen
A weird and funny royal

But the Queen of Hearts
Is by far the worst
For day & night
She cries out
"Off with her head!"
"Off with his head!"

Alice painted roses
Went from square to square
Soon she became
A queen
But that's just the beginning

She returns
In time
For Frabjous Day
To slay the beast
That Jabberwocky
Saving the day
The Red Queen was banished
The White Queen now rules

And remember my friends
This tale is quite true
Who's the next Alice?
That will travel the land
Crafting the dream
Vorpal sword in hand
It could happen
A year from now
Maybe two
But who knows?
The next Alice
Could be…you

By Violetta Nagy

Saturday Morning

I open my eyes,
Saturday
I'm wide awake
But I stay in bed
And enjoy the comfort of it.
I enjoy the warmth
I enjoy not getting my sleep interrupted
I enjoy the sunlight shining in the room
I enjoy the quiet of the house
I enjoy
Saturday.

By Minki Ha

The Ninja Stalks His Prey

This is the ninja's last job, his employer will give him a lot of money for this, but this is big, the prey is a leader, a ruler, an emperor. The ninja has stalked for weeks; if he fails he will lose everything. The ninja is ready, phase one is in motion.

As morning breaks, the prey goes on his walk. The ninja stalks, thinking of his family… Everything is going well, the guards have been, "taken care of" for him. The emperor sits down on a rock, newt to a pond. The time is right. Phase two. The ninja creeps, moves closer, star in his hand. His wrist twitches, the deed is done.

Phase three. The ninja must evacuate, he finds a guard and takes his uniform, and his soul. The ninja is exited, but he has been trained to be calm, he has joined a troop of guards. The bells sound, the alarm is ringing, he is almost out. The doors are closing, the outside world slips away, but then he gets through. His troop went to guard the outside. The ninja is free, no more stalking, the job is completed. The employer is pleased, time to go home…

By Carl Dobrovic

Ode to Sleep

Ode to sleep.
You put me to rest,
You make me drowsy,
And rest me in haven.

You give me the warmth,
You make the dreams of happiness,
You give me everything I need,
The feeling of sleep.

And then I wake up,
Ready to go,
And at the end of the day,
You bring me back to sleep.

Ode to sleep.

By Daniel Shin

NBA

I stood looking at my Apple Mac
While playing basketball with Shaq
Kapow! I slipped I need my first aid
My pal helped me up "thanks D-Wade".
I turned around I saw Chris Bosh
He was screaming "Oh my gosh."
Chris Bosh has the hiccups
BOO! Chris got scared by Billups.
I hear the dribble from the ball
My friend stole the ball, "thanks Wall".
I was eating a beet
Then I saw the whole team of the Miami Heat.
My coach was yelling at me
"Shut up Doc Rivers."
All of a sudden I got the shivers.
There was a loud bid.
A mob was bidding for Jason Kidd.
I went on Bing.
BOOOM! Crashed Yao Ming.
My friend Rose
Was doing a cool pose.
There was Boozer acting cool.
He is such a loser.

My head was on flames.
My bro washed it with water
"thanks LeBron James."
I was living in a condo.
With my friend Rondo.
I saw the Navy.
They were arresting Big Baby.
Where amazing Happens.

By Alex Shin

The Perfect Book
I open the book,
Wondering
"How will it be?"
I remember
One book
It wasn't for me
I couldn't get through

But this book,
Was not like that one
No
Not in the least
This one
Was my book
The perfect book

The magic
The romance
The action
I couldn't put it down
Pages
Of paradise

And then I saw the back
Cover
And realized
It was finished
The sorrow
Was too much to bear

For I live off of books
And I still do

So I put down the old book
Picked up a new
And began to read
again

By Shruti Ray

Ode to Chocolate
I devour you
In my mouth
Your rich taste
Leaves me tingling
With joy
Oh, chocolate…
How could I live without you
You're like a warm blanket
When I feel cold and sad
I bite you
And my mouth explodes with
Happiness
Your dark brown color
And rich creamy insides….
What a beauty you are
Oh, chocolate….
Your sparkly silver wrapping,
Is like a present
When I open you, I feel like a little kid
On Christmas morning
When I get my hands on you
I just want to devour your beauty
And love you,
Forever
Chocolate
You
Are
My true
Love

By Arleigh Kritsky

The Key

Today things happen
That I may or may not
Remember
In a while
I'll lose the key to get it back

It's there
I just can't
find it

By Sarah Goswick

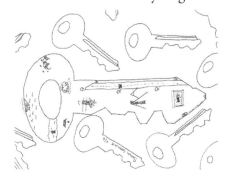

Cat vs. Dog

There sits a cat
Drinking its milk
On a mat
That is soft as silk

But then comes a dog
Ready for war
Looking at the cat
Starting to soar

Through the air
Though the dog doesn't care
Because... SPLAT
The dog moved out the way
The cat hit the wall
Hurray

But the cat gets right up
Pulls out a machete
And chops the dog up
Into streams of spaghetti

The dog starts to bleed
On the mat of silk
It's really disgusting
Then...
The cat goes back to drinking its milk

By Iain Allingham

Writers Block

I pick up a pencil
And have nothing to say
My idea goes poof
And floats away

My brain goes empty
I am bored to my skull
What should I write about?
Something small or tall?

Should I write about fairies?
Or dragons with fire?
Or should I write about,
My dad's rusty tire?

Writing is not my thing
For I love to talk
I always seem to have
Writers block.

By Ellie Gosling

The Wolves Are Coming

It is night.
The wolves are coming,
To catch their prey.
Many are in a slumber.
A wolf's glare,
Starts the hunting.

The predators are hunting,
During the night.
The wolves piercing glare,
Shows that it is coming.
During the prey's slumber,
The wolf catches its prey.

A wolf catches some prey,
Then it howls and resumes its hunting.
The wolves catch a rabbit in its slumber.
Stealthy in the darkness of night,
It's coming
It stares at me with its piercing glare.

It starts to glare,

And runs after its prey.
A new pack is coming
To join the hunting.
In the shadows of night,
A wolf catches prey that was in a slumber

It ends as animals rise from slumber

By Robert Durst

Untitled

abstract art
it catches the eye
and pulls it in
then when you get close
it scares you away
over the days after you saw it
the image plays in your mind
tempting you to study it
finally you give in
and when you study it
it brings you into
a colorful
blissfulness

By Joshua Laney

Gatorade

After I work so hard
And sweat and sweat
You replenish
The feel of you in my mouth
You quench
The long needed thirst
With your
Excellent taste
That cool rush of
Flavor
Going down my throat
As I take another
Sip
And I hear that gulp
I look at the bottle
And see
It is empty
Sadness fills me
Oh Gatorade
Perfect is you

By Theo Lenz

Sixth Grade
Mrs. Rossbach

Glistening Delight
Falling moon in light
Stillness fills the air
Shimmering in sight
glistening delight
By Leah Harriman

A Wooded Land
A wooded land,
covered completely by trees
Light filled up the spaces
in between the branches
A girl strode down a
winding pathway, when a
hawk called out into
the crisp air, looking
for food

A stampede of lords
and ladies on horses
filled the air with the
sound of pounding hooves
The girl hid behind the
fingers of a knurled oak
the story teller
the old one

The day was ending
the old, wise owl
called out into the night
spreading his wings
and soaring
diving through the foliage
in search of provisions for his family
the owl headed back
to his tree as a dusting
of light came into
the sky
a chickadee called out "the day has come!
Wake up!"
The singing of birds
filled the air
conversations buzzing noisily

The sun hiked up into the sky
bringing bright blue
a stream gurgled
a creek bubbled
and the trees watched
peacefully
By Elizabeth Eareckson

Funny Joint
The things I find Funny,
People don't laugh,
Things I don't find funny,
People always laugh,
The funny thing is when,
I find things funny people laugh…. Sometimes
By Manuel Madrid

A Feeble Flame

A candle flickers in the breeze,
twisting and turning
this way and that.
Its flame licks up
the surrounding darkness
in each swift movement
as it steadily glimmers.
A tear of wax slithers down its side,
tripping ever so often
with its unsteady pace.
It reflects on the time
when adventures could be taken
and problems could be overcome.
But now as he waits,
too old to go back,
and too young to move forward,
his past shivers through him,
shattering the luminous steady heat
and instead turning it into
a blazing flame of rage.
His thoughts sting through him
as he recalls all the perilous events
that caused so much hardship
throughout his life.
Confusion and guilt
dash through his soul,
rushing to seize each untaken location.
His shattered heart
taunts him over and over again,
torturing his frail mind.
A young and delicate moth,
mesmerized by the dim radiance of the candle
sits and waits for something to happen.
The glowing blaze smiles to himself
and envy's the innocent creature
who has not yet done right or wrong.
He whispers to it,
"Don't let yourself fall…"
and watches as it flutters away
leaving a quiet trail of dust
where it had been sitting.
And gazing at that trail of dust,
The candle brings back trust
and faith into his cold worn heart.
And he tells himself,
I'm not afraid to die…
repeatedly even though he knew he was.
"I'm not afraid to die"
Again
each time saying it stronger,
louder than before.
Each time,
becoming more certain of his words.
Until he was shouting to the open air
again and again
as if proving himself to the Gods.
"I'm not afraid to die!"
And he laughed.
The greatest,
most devastating laugh,
that echoed through the open air.
And even through this overwhelming time,
he was able
to gain back the slivers of good memories,
the ones that had untangled
all the strain
and let him enjoy what he had.
With all his miserable joy,
he called for the winds
and allowed them
to swirled around his chilled body.
Flickering and flickering,
the candle waits,
until the glorious flame
suddenly vanished out of sight,
leaving behind nothing,
but an empty lifeless candlestick
with a thread of smoke rising up,
weaving through the midnight sky.

By Mina H Mohtasham

Apocalypse

It is the apocalypse
And I have caught a glimpse
Of a devastated world
It is burning up
All around us
You hear screams and fire
And there is no way out
The flames have reached
A record high height
Moms are screaming, Dads are yelling and babies are crying
Until you wake up
and it was only just a dream

By Jacob Cole

Forgiving Wrongs Forever

After pain from people
Abandonment
The nerve of them coming back
Asking for another chance
Is angering
Trust
Starts to wither away
The number of chances
Is quickly
Running out
Tolerance
Is fading
Anger rises
Patience is leaving
With thoughtful feelings
Giving
And never receiving
Is starting to rub you
The wrong way
But with regret
You forgive them
Again

By Clhoe Billups

Four Quarters

If I had a quarter for each season in a year
It would be worth a dollar
And if I had a dollar for every year I'd lived
My life would be worth twelve
But a year is worth so much more than
just four quarters
Which is the number of seasons in a year
Because each season brings things
that money can't buy
Like the wind whispering through
the willows in spring
Or the snow that falls lightly
on the ground in the cold winters
The laughter of children in the summer
Or the crackling of leaves as you
walk through the woods in fall
If life was worth just four quarters
All this would mean nothing
If life was worth just four quarters
There would be no reason for us to have those
four little quarters if we wasted them
Because you've only got one life to live
And it's worth more than anything
money can buy
I don't know about you but my life I'd rather
spend out underneath the sky
Because life is worth so much more
than four little quarters
That's the truth I tell, but you have to decide

By Olivia Wisnewski

Name

What is my name?
Why do I need a name?
What does name mean?
What if I didn't have a name?
Would I survive?
Are we all just playing a name game?
When will this game end?

By: Unknown (Abby Torres)

If the cow jumped over the moon...

If the cow jumped over the moon
where did he learn to fly?
If the cow jumped over the moon
why did he not just die?
If the cow jumped over the moon
he probably just faked it.
If the cow jumped over the moon
he surely could not make it.
If the cow jumped over the moon
he would have to jump really high.
If the cow jumped over the moon
he could jump off the Burg Dubai.
If the cow jumped over the moon
he could take a spaceship.
If the cow jumped over the moon
I hope he did not skip.
If the cow jumped over the moon
he did it with flying cars.
If the cow jumped over the moon
why didn't he go to Mars?
The cow did not jump over the moon
for it would have gone wrong.
(Please do sing this because it is not a song).

By Teddy Huffer

Paper Airplanes

They fly in any which way
The breeze is like a shove of power
The folds and creases are bent perfectly
The tips are sharp as daggers
The little boy lets the plane fly through
The damp wind
Crunch the leaves go
As he walks
Through the woods
To find
His abandoned plane
Perched on a tall branch
Waiting for another launch

By Phoebe Warstler

Cold as Ice

The owl's shadow soars across
the glowing moon.
Now I know that the brutal winter is
here to stay.
A gust of wind hits me.
I turn my cheek with a shade of light red.
As I walk to the door to go inside,
I'm as cold as ice.

By Nicholas Duran

Gasping Seagulls

Gaping their mouths
Bursting through air
Fighting for fish
Feathers everywhere
Floating in blue
Trying their luck
Snatching bread crumbs
Gasping Seagulls

By Angela He

Narwals

Naughty & nice
Also seen on Youtube
Really long sharp thingy on face
Weird mix between unicorn & shark
Hilarious
Awesome
Lethargic
Super buff

By Jeffrey Turner

The Path of Success

I am slowly walking
This lonely path of success
Walking
On a lonely path
Of being the best
Stepping on others
Going alone
Watching others fall
At my own hands
Myself
Going on
At the fault of others
This is the lonely path
Of my own success

By Max Peters

The Summer Sun

The Summer Sun
Like a fiery gem
Golden yellow
Gleaming like a crystal
With brilliant radiance
Its golden rays of light
Light up the summer day
And shimmer on the grass
The Summer Sun
Shining down on the world

By Nitin Rao

Sock Eating Girl

The little girl, she
likes to eat socks

She jumps and hops and
takes them from my box

She runs and sprains and
growls and barks when
I come

She runs and hides and
so do I when she thinks
it's fun

She stole my heart and
she's my little dog

By: Rebecca Grundahl

The Proposal

They're at dinner,
He is ready to propose.
He's got to distract her,
By saying, "Why look at her nose."
She turns around,
He's on his knee.
He then says,
"Will you marry me?"
She panics.
She thinks about it,
Then she says,
"There's no doubt about it!"

Christian Adlam

Orca Whales

The orca whale is swimming
So gracefully through the ocean
It's shimmering, shining, smooth
Skin shining under the sun
It sees a fish and GULP
The fish is gone

By Nathan Gulakowski

The Surfer

The surfer
He waits
For the wave
To ride in
He sees the wave
To ride in
He starts to paddle
The wave catches him
He stands up
Oh no
Too late
So he tries again

By Robby Cordts

Winters White

The chill air withers the green that is still left
Dark fat puffy clouds block out the sun
We haven't splattered white yet though
The ground shrugs off the frost each morning
Only to do it again tomorrow
The trees moan in the winter gales
But we haven't been splattered white yet
So my fire still burns the frosted wood

By Ashton Reinhold

Words

So meaningful they take your breath away
Never ending
Sometimes
Words are just letters
All scrambled up
Away from order
But why?
Why do words hurt others?
They are just letters
How can plain letters
Hurt someone so badly?
Words can hurt
They are uncontrollable
In some ways
Sometimes
They slip through the gate
And attack
They leave the victim hurt and confused
Most letters are good
But scrambled up in the wrong order
Can cause hurt
And pain
What I am writing now
Are words
Scrambled up
And used to tell you
To use them carefully
Don't hurt others
By using letters
That are scrambled up
They are words
Words
Words

By Mikaela Walker

What if…?

What if there were such things as flying cars,
Or dolls with wheels, or aliens on Mars?
What if we could all read minds?
Or each have real crystals—all different kinds!
What if spaghetti could fall from the skies?
Or we could all get free Starbucks
every day of our lives!
Sure, it would be fun if we had everything,
But then what would we have
to look forward to?
Nothing!

By Emily Silverio

Books

Books books books read reading books
books books books
Books are a place to escape to
Books words swirling in my head
Books reading books books books books
Books painting a picture in my mind
Book a picture of stars
Books books books books reading books
books books books
Books words coming together to make a story
book books
Read book books books books books books
book books books

By Madison Silver

Sour Patch Kids!

Sour patch kids are good
Sour patch kids are goo
Sour patch kids are go
Sour patch kids are g
Sour patch kids are
Sour patch kids ar
Sour patch kids a
Sour patch kids
Sour patch kid
Sour patch ki
Sour patch k
Sour patch
Sour patc
Sour pat
Sour pa
Sour p
Sour

By WilliamMartin

No Time

I'm always here
I'm always here
But then I have not time to spare!
1,2,3
4,5,6
When do I pick up the stick?
I cook
I clean
I sweep the floor
I really cannot do much more
And now I'm on the floor once more!

By Bailey Withers

Nature

I run outside with my dog at my heels
She runs in figure eights around the backyard
And crouches down with her tail wagging
Begging for a chase, my legs carry me
Across the backyard after her and
We run around

I slump down on the fresh, green grass
And as Slinky plops down next to me, I run
My fingertips through the short, soft fur on
Top of her head
Her tongue lolls out as she rests
And she puts her head on my lap

The grass tickles the underside of my hand
Trying to make me laugh and pull my hand away
The breeze blows back my hair and jingles the
toys on Slinky's collar

I lean back into the fresh, green grass and rest,
Knowing that Slinky is beside me
And nature is all around me

I shut my eyes and I listen to the sparrow chirp,
the cardinal call
The robin stretches its wings and soars overhead
Singing to us as it goes by
The birds flit by and watch us rest
And as they go through
the emerald leaves of the trees
they tweet and chirp and wonder why we sit

Nature is all around me, so I lean back and rest
I am lulled to sleep by the smells, sounds, feelings, and comforts of
Nature

By Elisa Nicolini

The Typing Dog

So there's a dog
Right?
But he wears glasses
High end business glasses
And shoes
Polished business shoes

And then he sits

On a chair
That swirls
Which is on wheels
But when he sits
He sits like a man
Not a dog
With his feet dangling on the side of his chair
His back up right

And then he rolls up to a desk
A business desk
That was custom made
For him
Made of polished mahogany
A picture of his puppies in the corner

Kinda weird....
And then there's a laptop
On the desk
An apple computer...

And then his paws go up
Onto the desk
And then on the keyboard
He coughs
And starts typing
A business deal
His paws moving like the wind
On the key board....

Awkward....

By Bryce Onozuka

Made in the USA
Charleston, SC
08 June 2011